SECOND EDITION

Linked in
UNLOCKED

D1518332

GET YOUR FREE GIFT

The LinkedIn Unlocked Resource Pack provides all the exercises, checklists, and templates (and more) presented in this book. **It's yours FREE to download at:**
LinkedinUnlockedBook.com
Use the secret word: *Bonus*

ISBN: 9798861778732

Bulk discounts are available to use as promotions or for corporate LinkedIn and social selling training programs.

For details email: info@topdogsocialmedia.com

SECOND EDITION

Linked in
UNLOCKED

U NLOCK THE MYSTERY OF
LINKEDIN TO DRIVE MORE SALES
THROUGH SOCIAL SELLING

MELONIE DODARO

PRAISE FOR LINKEDIN UNLOCKED

"Filled with practical advice and eye-opening tips, this is the 'user's manual' for LinkedIn you'll wish you had years ago. Highly recommended."

JAY BAER, New York Times bestselling author

"This book covers every aspect of social selling and how you can use LinkedIn to your advantage. Don't just read this book, implement it."

JEFFREY GITOMER, New York Times bestselling author

"In *LinkedIn Unlocked*, Melonie Dodaro shares her method for abandoning the old ways of selling and embracing LinkedIn as a powerful tool to generate leads that lead to sales."

MICHAEL STELZNER, CEO of Social Media Examiner

"Brilliant! Melonie has written a very practical, how-to course in a book. I especially love the social selling framework. I'm recommending *LinkedIn Unlocked* to all my clients!"

MARI SMITH, bestselling author

"In *LinkedIn Unlocked*, Melonie gives you the roadmap to activating the digital rolodex that is LinkedIn. Her practical approach to social selling will help you turn digital profiles into real-life connections and new business."

EKATERINA WALTER, Wall Street Journal bestselling author

"It's rare that you come across a great book about LinkedIn, but Melonie has nailed it with *LinkedIn Unlocked*! Enormously helpful for anyone who wants to leverage the power of LinkedIn to achieve more leads, clients, and sales."

KIM GARST, bestselling author

"Melonie has done it again with *LinkedIn Unlocked*, providing a step-by-step process of how to combine LinkedIn with social selling, attract more clients, and add more to your bottom line."

JOEL COMM, New York Times bestselling author

"*LinkedIn Unlocked* could also be called Sales Unlocked! Read this book and follow Melonie's proven formula and you are guaranteed to increase sales for your business."

IAN CLEARY, founder of RazorSocial

"Responsive. Highly Pragmatic. Results Driven. A handful of words that immediately come to mind when I think of Melonie Dodaro. Her approach with *LinkedIn Unlocked* and social selling is second to none!"

REBEKAH RADICE, founder of RadiantLA

"*LinkedIn Unlocked* is a complete lead generation and revenue acceleration seminar, all in one book. Don't miss this opportunity to get inside Melonie's savvy mind for social selling and take action on what you learn in this book!"

DONNA MORITZ, CEO of Socially Sorted

"If anyone can unlock the secrets, again, to utilizing LinkedIn to their advantage, it's Melonie in *LinkedIn Unlocked*. Don't miss this latest opportunity to learn from the best. Relationships are like muscle tissue, the more you engage them, the stronger and more valuable they become."

TED RUBIN, bestselling author

"Melonie is spot-on! She shares the 'how to' of social selling while reinforcing it's about building relationships. If you're looking for a way to generate leads on LinkedIn, and grow in value to your network, then you must get *LinkedIn Unlocked*."

AJ WILCOX, CEO of B2Linked

"Melonie's proprietary formula outlined in *LinkedIn Unlocked*, will not only help you increase your bottom line, but it will also assist you in attracting new clients for years to come!"

ALLISON MASLAN, CEO of Pinnacle Global Network

"*LinkedIn Unlocked* shows you how to use LinkedIn to get directly in front of potential buyers. This is a must-read for any B2B individual, business or sales professional."

PERRY VAN BEEK, CEO of Social One

"Concise, practical, and universally relevant. Melonie has laid out a path for you in *LinkedIn Unlocked*. Follow it!"

ANDY CRESTODINA, CMO of Orbit Media

"If only there were a way to make *LinkedIn Unlocked* required reading before people reached out to me on LinkedIn. That would make me happy and open the door for successful new relationships."

STEVE DOTTO, host of Dotto Tech

"If you want to know how to leverage LinkedIn for more business, *LinkedIn Unlocked* is a must read. This book is filled with strategies that will help you attract leads and clients, ethically."

LISA LARTER, bestselling author

"In *LinkedIn Unlocked*, Melonie guides the reader to a 'how can I help you' mindset, which is crucial to success with modern buyers. A 'how can I help you' mindset is the only way to grow and develop relationships in today's business climate. A must-read for anyone in business."

VICTORIA TAYLOR, founder of Untwisted Media

"LinkedIn is one of the best tools we have at our disposal to make more sales—and there are few better at LinkedIn marketing than Melonie! If you're serious about social selling, read *LinkedIn Unlocked* asap."

LILACH BULLOCK, online business expert

"*LinkedIn Unlocked* is loaded with excellent information and is a must-read for inspired, forward-thinking professionals in search of the most effective social media methods to promote their business presence and sales revenues."

ANGUS GILLESPIE, editor-in-chief of *The Canadian Business Journal*

"*LinkedIn Unlocked* lays out a comprehensive, yet easy-to-implement plan to make a direct impact on your lead generation and conversion goals."

LISA JENKINS, editor of *Social Media Examiner*

"Smart, engaging, and relevant. Buy the book, then put it into practice."

BRYAN KRAMER, TED speaker and bestselling author

"Overdue and understated. *LinkedIn Unlocked* changes your thinking around social selling with a people-first approach. Melonie's modern selling techniques are well-advised, practical, and will return results that last."

JOANNE SWEENEY-BURKE, CEO of Digital Training Institute

"When I need to up my LinkedIn game, Melonie is my go-to resource! *LinkedIn Unlocked* is a complete social selling playbook to go beyond sharing content and hoping for results, to get a measurable and consistent ROI."

EMERIC ERNOULT, CEO of Agorapulse

"Lead generation on LinkedIn is no longer a mystery thanks to *LinkedIn Unlocked*. Melonie breaks down the exact steps to drive more sales with LinkedIn. Any business can take advantage of social selling; you just need to read this book and implement it."

SIGRUN GUDJONSDOTTIR, mastermind mentor and international speaker

"*LinkedIn Unlocked* should become your 'go to guide' for using LinkedIn to attract ideal prospects and generate sales. Don't just read it; implement what you learn and transform your business."

DYLIS GUYAN, sales and marketing leader

"In *LinkedIn Unlocked*, Melonie has once again delivered a balanced approach of sound principles and practical step-by-step advice any professional can deploy quickly. If you want to leverage LinkedIn as a business development tool, read and apply the great ideas in this book."

ED GANDIA, host of the High-Income Business Writing Podcast

"This is the roadmap to unlocking the power of LinkedIn we've all been waiting for."

HUGH CULVER, speaker and author

"*LinkedIn Unlocked* takes you through every step of the digital journey to reach your sales and revenue goals. The process is broken down into manageable and practical steps for anyone to achieve success."

MIC ADAM, CEO of Vanguard Leadership

"*LinkedIn Unlocked* is a remarkable tool in your social selling toolbox that gets to the heart of what matters: building real conversations and relationships, which result in increased sales."

DOYLE BUELER, CEO of Dept.Digital

"*LinkedIn Unlocked* is an actionable guidebook for those who want to leverage the power of LinkedIn to build their brand and their business."

PHIL GERBYSHAK, social selling trainer and speaker

"*LinkedIn Unlocked* is full of practical advice that can be easily implemented by anyone who is interested in building their personal brand. I've used Melonie's tips in my work with students and alumni to help them get a head start in their career."

RICHELLE MATAS, Alumni Relations at The University of British Columbia

"*LinkedIn Unlocked* completely removes the mystery of how to use LinkedIn as an effective tool for lead generation to grow your business."

SAMANTHA KELLY, founder of Women's Inspire Network

"*LinkedIn Unlocked* shares a powerful method and structure for using LinkedIn to attract, build, and create revenue for your business. Using her powerful methods, practical ideas, and honed advice, you can lay the foundation to develop and grow lasting and authentic relationships."

ALI MEEHAN, founder of Costa Women

"*LinkedIn Unlocked* articulates the power of LinkedIn and shows you exactly how to make the most of it. I'll be recommending to all my students and clients."

RENÉE VELDMAN-TENTORI, university lecturer

"You have to be careful when taking advice on social selling. The approach laid out in *LinkedIn Unlocked* shows you how to have authentic communication that builds relationships. You will avoid mistakes and learn a repeatable methodology that allows you to embrace LinkedIn as a selling tool."

BETH GRANGER, LinkedIn trainer and consultant

"Melonie Dodaro is an expert when it comes to unraveling the mysteries of social selling through LinkedIn. In *LinkedIn Unlocked*, she shares simple but strategic steps to increase sales through the power of building relationships."

PATTY FARMER, marketing and media strategist, international speaker

"*LinkedIn Unlocked* provides great business insights on exactly how to use LinkedIn to grow sales. It's a must-read."

SAM GOLDFARB, CEO of Tradimax

"Melonie has once again demystified LinkedIn. Her keen insights into this powerful, yet often misunderstood tool, extend well beyond mere technical applications. A must-read for anyone who wants to leverage the power of LinkedIn."

BEN ROBINSON, founder of Bookkeeper Business Launch

"*LinkedIn Unlocked* takes the mystery out of social selling on LinkedIn. Read it then put these techniques into action and watch your influence— and your sales—amplify!"

MELANIE BENSON, host of the Amplify Your Success Podcast

"*LinkedIn Unlocked* is not a book; it's a code for unlocking client-getting strategies that work today, delivered in a practical, step-by-step guide."

ADAM URBANSKI, CEO of Marketing Mentors

"With *LinkedIn Unlocked*, you have an unfair advantage in creating valuable and profitable relationships. Follow this proven formula that will stand the test of time, regardless of any changes to social media."

SABRINA GIBSON, CEO of Social Success Academy

"Everything you need to know to use LinkedIn for business successfully, is broken down into bite-size steps in *LinkedIn Unlocked*. The book, the process, and methods are all brilliant!"

PETRA FISHER, LinkedIn trainer and consultant

"This book will transform—yes, transform, that's the key word there— the way you think about LinkedIn as a tool and about the whole selling process. *LinkedIn Unlocked* provides the methodology of effective social selling plus an entire step-by-step guide on how to do it."

PAUL SKAH, four-time TEDx speaker and author

"If generating more leads and clients is your goal, then *LinkedIn Unlocked* is the handbook. It is a must read for all sales and business development teams."

JOHN ASHCROFT, CEO of Pro Manchester

"When I think of Melonie Dodaro, I think of her authenticity and ability to cultivate trust and genuine relationships. In *LinkedIn Unlocked*, she provides an actual strategy to drive sales in a world promising quick fixes that don't work."

LAURA TUCKER, leadership coach

"Melonie has done it again with her new book *LinkedIn Unlocked*. She pulls the curtain back and reveals the true value of investing in LinkedIn for social selling."

JOHN DALE BECKLEY, founder of Canary PR

"If you want a predictable stream of new leads and clients from LinkedIn, then *LinkedIn Unlocked* is a must read. This book is a game changer."

JULIA BRAMBLE, social media strategist

"*LinkedIn Unlocked* is the ultimate reference for LinkedIn marketing and lead generation! Melonie's LINK Method™ is an actionable and easy to implement plan that guarantees success."

ANTONIO CALERO, marketer

"*LinkedIn Unlocked* is filled with actionable tips and processes to connect with your audience and more importantly, to generate leads and more sales. It's a must-have manual for all business owners!"

IAN ANDERSON GRAY, founder of Seriously Social

"It's time to stop preparing to do the work and simply follow the social selling playbook laid out for you in *LinkedIn Unlocked*. It's got the Sales DNA that you need to generate more clients and sales."

PATRICK MARSHALL, TEC Canada chair

"*LinkedIn Unlocked* shows you exactly how to use LinkedIn and the art of relationship marketing to achieve real business results."

MIKE ALTON, brand evangelist at Agorapulse

"Melonie Dodaro has been one of my go-to LinkedIn experts for years! *LinkedIn Unlocked* takes the reader by the hand and, not only explains how LinkedIn works, but also shows you how to shine with an actionable roadmap."

HEIDI COHEN, author of *Actionable Marketing Guide*

SECOND EDITION

Linked in
UNLOCKED

UNLOCK THE MYSTERY OF
LINKEDIN TO DRIVE MORE SALES
THROUGH SOCIAL SELLING

MELONIE DODARO

CONTENTS

Introduction   1

PART ONE: FOUNDATIONS   5

CHAPTER ONE: The Power of LinkedIn for Business Growth   7
CHAPTER TWO: Identify Your Ideal Clients for Emotional Connection   21
CHAPTER THREE: Transform Your LinkedIn Profile to Attract Clients   31
CHAPTER FOUR: Compare LinkedIn Subscriptions for Full Potential   59

PART TWO: STRATEGIES   79

CHAPTER FIVE: Master LinkedIn Etiquette and Best Practices   81
CHAPTER SIX: Find Leads and Prospects on LinkedIn   97
CHAPTER SEVEN: Convert Connections to Clients with The LINK Method™   121

PART THREE: EXECUTION   141

CHAPTER EIGHT: Impactful Content to Increase Reach and Influence   143
CHAPTER NINE: Authority Building with AI-Enhanced Tailored Content   167
CHAPTER TEN: Ready-to-Launch Action Plan for Social Selling on LinkedIn   181

Conclusion   195
About The Author   199
Additional Resources   201
Index   203

INTRODUCTION

Over the years, I've found myself in numerous crowded conference and networking events. Heart racing, palms sweaty, I'd watch as people around me easily engaged in animated conversations and seamless networking. I was there too, but instead of enthusiastic handshakes and lively chats, my interactions were often limited to polite but detached smiles. If you're an introvert, you probably understand the energy and mental focus it takes to navigate events like these.

Understanding the importance of networking for my business, I regularly attended these events in the early years despite the discomfort and mental drain. I pushed myself to perform on the spot, mimicking the easy charisma of the extroverts around me. Yet, despite my efforts, I would come away from each gathering feeling mentally exhausted and defeated, questioning whether this was the only route to professional growth.

This struggle led me to explore alternatives, and that's when I found LinkedIn. This platform stood out as a meaningful alternative in the world of social media, far less chaotic and more business-oriented than Facebook, Instagram, TikTok, and the rest. As an introvert, I realized that LinkedIn provided a unique opportunity. Unlike the high-stakes environment of face-to-face networking events, LinkedIn allowed me to carefully curate my professional persona from the comfort of my own home.

I abandoned the need for high-pressure showmanship. Instead, I focused on building relationships at my own pace, offering valuable insights through written content. Leveraging the platform's features, I could now put my strengths in one-on-one communication and skill-building to good use.

The result was a transformation, from feeling drained to feeling energized and empowered. LinkedIn enabled me to establish myself as an industry thought leader and build a robust network without the associated stress or anxiety. It became my niche for business growth.

The aim of this updated edition of *LinkedIn Unlocked* is twofold. First, I want to empower introverts with the tools to thrive on this platform. Second, I want to provide a playbook that is equally effective for extroverts looking for a better way to network and generate high-quality leads.

It's vital to recognize that LinkedIn is not just evolving—it's undergoing a seismic shift. While its foundational role as an unparalleled tool for lead generation and relationship building remains consistent, the rules of the game have been completely rewritten. Tactics and strategies once effective are now obsolete, outpaced by rapidly-changing features, algorithms, and user behavior, rendering old lead generation methods ineffective.

This isn't just about "keeping up;" it's about adopting an entirely new playbook. This second edition of *LinkedIn Unlocked* serves as your navigational map through these uncharted waters, ensuring you're not just current, but ahead of the curve.

Since the first edition's release in 2018, LinkedIn has evolved significantly. While the essence of relationship building remains the same, the strategies to achieve it have dramatically changed. This is particularly crucial for small businesses and B2B service providers aiming to capture leads and secure new clients. With nearly a billion users globally, LinkedIn offers an unparalleled potential for targeted, meaningful connections.

But maximizing this potential isn't about casual participation; it requires a tailored strategy. That's where this updated edition shines. It's not just a guide;

it's your comprehensive playbook tailored to your networking style, whether you're an introvert or an extrovert, a LinkedIn novice or a seasoned pro.

In these pages, I will show you how to:

- Craft an irresistible profile that conveys credibility and invites trust
- Generate compelling content that positions you as an industry leader
- Build sustainable relationships that convert contacts into high-value clients
- Implement a LinkedIn sales system to supercharge your lead generation

While the technology behind LinkedIn will undoubtedly continue to evolve, the art of forming genuine human connections remains timeless. The strategies outlined in this book—infused with real relationship-building principles—provide a foolproof formula for LinkedIn success.

So, whether you're a newcomer to LinkedIn or you've been leveraging this platform for years, whether you identify as an introvert or an extrovert, this revised and expanded edition of *LinkedIn Unlocked* equips you with the most current, effective strategies to transform LinkedIn into your most powerful sales and marketing asset.

Follow this three-step framework and I guarantee you will increase your leads and sales:

1. **Read with Intent:** Don't just skim through the chapters. Approach each one with a focus on real-world application. Implement the profile enhancements, content strategies, and messaging guidelines as you go along, thereby systematically growing your presence and strengthening your relationships on LinkedIn

2. **Execute the Action Plans:** At the close of each chapter, you'll find action plans laid out in a step-by-step manner. These are not mere suggestions; they're your roadmap to transforming each chapter's insights into concrete results.

3. **Build Your Authority:** Combine the tactics in this book with your own unique skills and experiences to position yourself as an authority in your niche.

By following this framework, not only will you rise above your competition, you'll also turn LinkedIn into an invaluable business asset, a powerful channel for generating high-quality leads and impactful connections.

The strategies, insights, and action plans are all here, waiting for you.

PART ONE

FOUNDATIONS

CHAPTER ONE

The Power of LinkedIn for Business Growth

Do you remember when LinkedIn was merely a place where people posted their resume? It was something you set up and then promptly forgot. Yes, those were indeed simpler times. Fast-forward to today, and LinkedIn has transformed dramatically. It's no longer just a static, virtual CV depot. Instead, it has remade itself into a potent business tool. It has become a pillar for growth, a platform that B2B businesses would be wise not to overlook.

The digital transformation we have witnessed in our lifetimes regarding buying and selling cannot be ignored. In today's world, prospects have higher expectations than ever before. Think about the last time you received an unsolicited phone call, voicemail, or email from someone you didn't know. Did you respond? Most people don't. To succeed at using LinkedIn you must prioritize forming, building, and nurturing strong relationships with prospects and clients.

The key to personalized and meaningful engagement is understanding the value your prospects are looking for. This sets the stage for better outcomes, and builds trust. Cold calling and repetitive emails no longer serve as effective engagement strategies for modern buyers. Today's consumers are drawn to people and businesses who demonstrate an understanding of their client base and provide personalized, client-centric experiences across all touchpoints.

Businesses offering personalized solutions convert sales two to three times faster than those that do not.

According to a report recently released by LinkedIn:

- LinkedIn drives more traffic to B2B blogs and sites than any other social media platform.
- Executives rate LinkedIn high on value gained from their social marketing initiatives.

The report goes on to state:

Professionals are not just coming to LinkedIn in vast numbers; they're engaging with a huge purpose. They're coming specifically to connect to networks, brands, and opportunities by engaging with high-quality content across the LinkedIn platform. This is a very different mindset and intent from other social media platforms.

The world's professionals come to LinkedIn for:

- Industry news
- Expert advice
- Career training
- Peer insights and recommendations
- Content published by LinkedIn's influencers

Connecting effectively with today's buyers requires a modern sales and marketing approach. For those new to LinkedIn marketing and social selling, this may initially seem daunting. Many people still don't tap into LinkedIn's full potential, viewing it as overly complex.

However, by breaking things down into simple, actionable steps, tapping into LinkedIn's power is very achievable. This book provides a strategic yet accessible roadmap to guide you through the process. With the right mindset and consistent effort, you can master modern marketing on LinkedIn.

Over the years, I have created just such a modern marketing and lead generation system using LinkedIn. I call it the LinkedIn Domination Formula. I will share with you exactly how and why it works. Throughout this book, I will take you through the various elements of the process I use for my private clients, and show you how you can use this proven formula for your business.

I have attempted to make this book as clear and concise as possible for beginners to understand and follow, while also making sure the most advanced LinkedIn users become even more efficient and effective using the network for lead generation.

Before jumping in and starting on this social selling journey, take a few minutes to familiarize yourself with the LinkedIn Domination Formula below, which will help you get a clear picture of what you can learn from this book and how it will help you become a successful modern marketer.

LinkedIn Domination Formula: Unlocking the Full Power of LinkedIn

In this book, you'll unlock LinkedIn's full potential through my comprehensive three-stage framework that converts connections into valuable clients. This sequential formula serves as your roadmap to open doors for networking, lead generation, and business growth on LinkedIn's massive platform. The formula is built upon three foundational stages:

Stage 1: Credibility

Construct a credible and influential profile that attracts attention and builds trust.

Stage 2: Authority

Develop an audience-aligned content strategy and consistently provide value to establish your expertise.

Stage 3: Conversion

Systematically convert connections into clients and tangible business opportunities.

By mastering this three-stage formula through step-by-step strategies, you'll gain the framework to fully capitalize on LinkedIn for networking, leads, and growth.

Now let's explore what's included in each stage.

Stage 1: Credibility – Laying the Foundation for Trust

In this first, pivotal stage, you'll construct a rock-solid foundation of credibility that fuels trust. This involves optimizing your profile for maximum visibility, engagement, and appeal to your ideal clients. It involves the following steps:

- **Identifying Your Target Audience and Goals**: Understand your ideal client's pain points and challenges and establish clear goals to track your progress in serving this audience.
- **Profile Mastery**: Create an irresistibly engaging profile tailored to your audience by optimizing for attention, audience alignment, and approachability.
- **Boosting Your Visibility**: Take a proactive approach to maximizing the visibility of your profile and content using LinkedIn's unique algorithms.
- **Showcasing Social Proof**: Validate your expertise and build credibility through social proof elements, such as skill endorsements, recommendations, and reputation highlights.

By mastering Stage 1, you'll set up a credibility-rich profile designed to build trust and convert your network into business opportunities.

Stage 2: Authority – Increasing Your Influence

Stage 2 is all about converting visibility into bona fide influence by positioning yourself as an authority. It consists of:

- **Defining Your Content Strategy**: Create a strategic framework for content that resonates with your audience, by focusing on audience alignment, the optimal format, and maintaining a consistent publishing schedule.
- **Crafting Value-Based Content**: Step into your role as a go-to industry resource by generating actionable, problem-solving content that speaks directly to your target market.
- **Implementing an Engagement Plan**: Fuel your influence through purposeful audience engagement, and relationship building.

By taking a strategic approach to creating and promoting value-based content, you will establish yourself as an industry authority.

Stage 3: Conversion – Fueling Your Sales Engine

The final stage pivots your LinkedIn activities toward actionable business opportunities, utilizing strategies such as:

- **Mastering LinkedIn Messaging**: Learn to spark interest and build meaningful relationships through tailored, strategic messaging.
- **Implementing Lead Nurturing**: Employ follow-up sequences and optimal timing to sustain engagement with not-yet-ready prospects.
- **Creating a Consistent Action Plan**: Systematize your daily and weekly LinkedIn activities, and create an offline transition strategy, for executing high-impact messaging and follow-ups.

- **Tracking Performance and Continual Improvement**: Use key metrics and results monitoring to continually refine and optimize your approach.

By adopting a strategic approach to LinkedIn messaging and relationship-building, you can create a reliable sales pipeline on the platform—one that consistently transforms connections into meaningful conversations and, ultimately, into loyal clients.

By the time you reach the final chapter of this book, you'll be fully prepared to dominate LinkedIn. You'll know how to leverage its powerful features to gain credibility, establish authority, and drive conversions. So get ready to excel using each step of this proven formula.

Understanding Today's Modern Buyers

Our world is much different than it was even just five years ago, and it's exponentially different than it was just one year ago because of the transformations that have occurred with artificial intelligence. This is because we have evolved, as have our habits, matching the evolution of our technology.

The adoption of this technology is far and wide, with recent compelling statistics like these:

- 80% of B2B leads coming from social media are from LinkedIn. (Source: Oktapost)
- 97% of B2B marketers use LinkedIn to help drive their content marketing strategy. (Source: CMI)
- 93% of B2B content marketers use LinkedIn for organic social marketing. (Source: LeadsBridge)
- Businesses that prioritize social selling are 51% more likely to reach their sales quota. (Source: LinkedIn's State of Sales report)

- Audiences exposed to brand messages on LinkedIn are 6 times more likely to convert. (Source: HubSpot)
- 31% of sales reps using social selling reported closing deals worth over $500,000 without a single in-person meeting with the buyer. (Source: LinkedIn's State of Sales report)
- Brands get 7 times more reactions and 24 times more comments on LinkedIn Live streams than regular video. (Source: LinkedIn)
- Companies that post weekly on LinkedIn see double the engagement rate. (Source: LinkedIn)

These statistics highlight the significant role that LinkedIn plays in sales and marketing. They also demonstrate the effectiveness of social selling on LinkedIn and the impact it can have on sales outcomes. Understanding these preferences is key to building relationships with modern buyers and staying ahead in this rapidly evolving environment.

The methods through which today's modern buyers access information have evolved alongside technology. The COVID-19 pandemic accelerated this evolution, altering our buying habits and heightening our expectations for personalization from companies. Even small and medium-sized businesses are tailoring their online engagement to cater to these demands. It's essential to understand that today's modern buyers are primarily digital buyers who engage in online social networks to research companies and get recommendations. To stay competitive, you must educate yourself, build relationships, and connect with your buyers digitally to better understand their expectations from you and what they are truly looking for.

A New Sales Dialogue: Value-Based Selling

The sales dialogue has shifted toward value-based selling. It's no longer about "what can I sell you?" but rather "how can I help you?" This approach signals that you care about the client and their business and are consistently seeking ways to add value to their lives. Adopting this mindset is key to successful social selling. Understanding buyer psychology is critical to effectively incorporating this method into your social selling strategy.

To effectively transition from selling to helping, it's essential to address your prospects biggest question: "What's in it for me?" Failing to answer this leads to challenges in showcasing enough value through your sales process. Most objections come from a lack of belief in the value of your offer. If a prospect is convinced of the value they will receive, they will buy with enthusiasm.

To truly offer value, it's crucial to understand what matters most to your audience. Their motivations, either professional or personal, will be evident from the nature of their questions. It's also important to recognize that people use both emotion and logic to make decisions. Client-centric stories, such as case studies and testimonials, are one of the best ways to provide prospects with the ability to connect with your offer both emotionally and logically.

Your prospects often have two types of needs: functional and emotional. Understanding both allows you to position your product or service in a way that addresses both. By understanding buyer psychology, you can effectively communicate your value, position your product or service to address both functional and emotional needs, and ultimately drive more sales.

The Business Case for Building Trust

In the world of B2B products and services, trust is the main factor influencing buyers' decision-making processes. Yes, you read that correctly—trust is even more important than price. Hence, a value-based selling approach is essential in building trust. The concept is straightforward: if people trust you and know you have the solution they're looking for, they'll buy from you. But if they don't trust you, they won't even give you the time of day, let alone their hard-earned cash.

So, let's talk about the economy of trust. Today, trust must be at the forefront of all businesses' minds, and deeply integrated into their digital and social selling strategies. Why? Because trust is becoming increasingly absent in the world of business, and people are talking about it more and more. Warren Buffett once said, "Trust is like the air we breathe—when it's present, nobody really notices. When it's absent, everyone notices."

Here are some trust-building strategies you can start using right away:

- **Be authentic in your interactions.** Authenticity is key to building trust with prospects through social selling. Avoid gimmicky or disingenuous messages, and be sure that the messages you send are similar to what you would say if the person was standing in front of you. If you are using AI to craft messages, be sure to edit it well to add that missing human element.
- **Be transparent.** Always be honest and open about your business practices, pricing, terms, and conditions. No one likes surprises, at least not in business.
- **Listen and observe.** Engage in social listening to get to know your prospects, their challenges, desires, and communication style.
- **Provide excellent customer service.** Respond promptly to inquiries, provide useful information, and resolve issues quickly and effectively.
- **Be genuine with your engagement.** When engaging with prospects, comment thoughtfully and genuinely. Sincerity is key, and prospects will spot a lack of it from a mile away.

By fostering trust with your prospects, you can differentiate yourself from your competitors, reduce sales cycles, and win more deals. Trust is the foundation of any successful digital and social selling strategy, so focus on building it and watch your revenue soar.

Defining Social Selling

Social selling is all about building relationships with potential leads and clients using social media platforms and digital tools. Unlike traditional sales methods, social selling prioritizes establishing a rapport with prospects over delivering generic sales pitches. It has plenty of noteworthy advantages, including particularly significant benefits:

- **Discover new high-quality leads:** Social selling involves researching and uncovering insights about the needs and priorities of prospects, which can reveal new leads. You can leverage mutual relationships to connect with decision-makers, dramatically improving the chances of a successful sale.

- **Increase conversions:** With better insights into the priorities of today's consumers and decision-makers, you have more information available to you to close more deals and develop long-term clients.

- **Drive bigger deals and greater revenue:** Social selling allows you to develop robust, valuable human connections with multiple people within a company, reaching a broader audience without becoming generic. Building stronger relationships can lead to significant growth opportunities, and having relationships with multiple people in a company leads to larger deals.

Social Selling = Relationship Building

The traditional approach to sales, such as cold calling and unsolicited emails, lost its effectiveness a long time ago. According to studies conducted by LinkedIn, 90% of decision-makers state that they will not buy from these approaches. Therefore, social selling has become an essential part of B2B sales, with 75% of buyers and 84% of C-level executives using social media to make purchasing decisions.

LinkedIn has become the go-to platform for researching and exchanging information on vendors and their products/services. In today's market, where competition is fierce, providing valuable content and insights to potential clients is essential for success. Without engaging in social selling, businesses risk losing out on potential sales to competitors who are building relationships with these potential clients online. By embracing social selling, businesses can stay ahead of the competition and increase their chances of converting leads into loyal clients.

The term "social selling" has always been misleading, suggesting that you connect with someone and begin immediately with a sales pitch, which could not be further from the truth. For this reason, LinkedIn has recently embraced the term "deep sales," which is exactly what I am teaching throughout this book.

For the purpose of this book, I will be using the term "social selling" rather than "deep sales," as it is a term more widely known and used. But make no mistake—what you learn throughout this book will be an approach to deep sales that will help you to reach your ideal clients and make an impact on them.

What is Your LinkedIn Quotient, and Why Should You Care?

Much like IQ (intelligence quotient) and EQ (emotional intelligence quotient), your LinkedIn Quotient (LQ) represents your knowledge of and current results on LinkedIn. Your LQ measures how effectively you use LinkedIn for social selling. Determining your LQ can help you identify missed opportunities and understand the benefits of a more strategic LinkedIn approach.

Take this quick assessment to find out your current LQ, and target areas where you can improve. Read each of the questions below, and answer either *yes* or *no*. Count the number of *yes* responses to calculate your current LQ.

LINKEDIN QUOTIENT	YES	NO
1. My LinkedIn profile is client-centric and 100% complete.		
2. I've received recommendations and endorsements from clients.		
3. Potential clients are consistently viewing my LinkedIn profile.		
4. I connect with new leads on LinkedIn regularly.		
5. I send personalized connection requests to any leads I'm interested in.		
6. Decision-makers accept my personalized connection requests.		
7. I follow leads I am attempting to sell to.		
8. I review what my leads are sharing and engage with their content.		
9. I share content on a consistent basis relevant to my target market.		
10. I am booking appointments with leads through LinkedIn.		
TOTAL		

Results (based on the total of *yes* answers):

8–10: High LQ
5–7: Moderate LQ
0–4: Low LQ

If you scored high, congratulations! You are already further ahead than the average person using LinkedIn for lead generation, but you still have many opportunities to take advantage of for even greater results. If you scored lower, don't worry. You can start immediately to strengthen your social selling skills and achieve greater success on LinkedIn with what you learn throughout this book.

The Social Selling Index

The Social Selling Index (SSI) is a useful set of metrics that can help in determining which areas of social selling are being done well and which could use improvement. It measures performance on a scale of 0–100 in four critical pillars: creating a professional brand, finding the right people, engaging with insights, and building strong relationships. According to LinkedIn, as a person's SSI rises, so does their sales success. However, it's important to treat the SSI as a measurement of progress in using LinkedIn rather than a guarantee of success.

Once your score is above 70, it's recommended to focus on doing only results-producing activities, such as building relationships with your current leads and clients. If your SSI score is below 70, particularly if it's below 50, it's important to set a goal to increase it over time by focusing on improving the biggest gaps in your lowest-scoring pillars first. The more you drive activities around these four areas, the higher your social selling index score will be.

- The first pillar, **create a professional brand**, reflects how well your LinkedIn profile represents your client's needs, and what kind of content you're publishing to establish credibility and authority.
- The second pillar, **find the right people**, reflects how well you are prospecting. Are you using LinkedIn's search and research tools efficiently?
- The third pillar, **engage with insights**, reflects how well you are creating and sharing valuable content that sparks conversations and strengthens relationships.

- Finally, the fourth pillar, **build strong relationships**, measures how successful you are at establishing trust and expanding your network by connecting with decision-makers.

It's important to note that the SSI score doesn't measure the quality of your activities or their impact on your ideal client. Therefore, it's essential to use the SSI score as a starting point to identify where to improve your LinkedIn usage.

ACTION PLAN

Now that you have a grasp of the power of LinkedIn for business growth, and the importance of social selling, it's time to gauge your starting point.

Step 1: Check Your SSI Score: Go to www.linkedin.com/sales/ssi to check your SSI score. Make a note of your overall score as well as your individual score for each of the four social selling pillars.

Step 2: Complete the LinkedIn Quotient Assessment: Complete the LinkedIn Quotient assessment provided in this chapter. Be honest with your answers—this is for your growth! Save or note down your starting LQ score. This will serve as a benchmark for your future progress.

As you move through the following chapters and implement the strategies discussed, you'll watch both your SSI and your LQ rise, reflecting your growing proficiency in leveraging LinkedIn for building a strong personal brand and generating new business.

CHAPTER TWO

Identify Your Ideal Clients for Emotional Connection

In the previous chapter you learned that the key to successful social selling is building relationships with your prospects. I will get to that in more detail; but first, it is essential to understand your target market. To begin, ask yourself the following questions:

- Who is your ideal client (and, more specifically, who are they on LinkedIn)?
- What is the typical language of their business, industry, or organization?
- What kinds of challenges do they face?

Throughout this chapter, you'll work on some exercises to help you answer these questions. Each exercise builds on the previous one, so take the time to complete each one in the order they are presented. From these exercises, gather the information, and use it improve your LinkedIn profile, write better lead generation messages, and create more interesting and valuable content.

Your Ideal Clients

Seth Godin once said, "Everyone is not your customer." Trying to sell your product or service to people who don't really need it can waste your time and energy. Instead, your goal should be to find the people who are most likely to buy your solution and who will benefit the most from it. If you try to market to everyone, you market to no one.

Even though you may be seeking prospects within a specific industry (where some generalities may be made), you are dealing with individuals from individual businesses. It is not the industry, company, or organization you are building a relationship with, but the individuals who make the decisions.

Your LinkedIn profile, the messages you send, and the content you create must be 100 percent client-centric. Show that you understand their problems and that you can offer a solution to solve them. If you understand where they're coming from, what their motivations are, and what language they speak, you'll be able to connect with them in a meaningful way.

Understanding Your Ideal Client

Defining your ideal client is a crucial first step in effectively marketing yourself. Let's go through a series of exercises to gain clarity on who this person is.

EXERCISE 1: Envision your perfect client

Imagine the perfect client for your product or service. What problems are they dealing with? How could you uniquely help them? Jot down your thoughts.

EXERCISE 2: Create an ideal client persona

Expand your vision of this ideal client into a tangible persona. Include details like job title and industry, company size and type, location, demographics, psychographics, interests, values, and personality. Fleshing out these details makes your ideal client more "real."

EXERCISE 3 : Identify commonalities among your best clients

Review your top 10 clients (past or present). What common threads do you notice in terms of role and industry, company traits, location, leadership style, and other similarities? Spotting patterns helps you hone in on your sweet spot.

Understanding Your Ideal Client's Pain Points and Needs

Now let's get into the mind of your ideal client. What challenges are they facing? How can you help?

EXERCISE 4 : Identify their problems

What specific problems and pain points are your ideal clients struggling with? These are issues they need resolved.

EXERCISE 5 : Discover the impact of the problems

How do these problems negatively impact your ideal client's business or personal life? Envision the ripple effect.

EXERCISE 6 : Uncover the worst-case scenarios

What are the worst-case scenarios if these problems remain unresolved? What's at stake for them?

EXERCISE 7 : Reveal what they stand to lose

What exactly could your ideal client lose if their problems persist? Money, time, reputation, relationships, peace of mind?

Defining your client's pain points creates empathy and shows how you can help. Now let's flip the script.

EXERCISE 8: Pinpoint their desired solution

How does your ideal client describe their perfect solution? What language do they use when describing it? Capture this.

EXERCISE 9: Envision their improved future state

How would your ideal client's business or personal life improve with the ideal solution in place? Expand your vision of their desired future state.

EXERCISE 10: Anticipate how they'll feel

What emotions would your ideal client feel if their problems were solved? Joy, confidence, pride, freedom? Describe their emotional state.

EXERCISE 11: Uncover their vision of perfection

Imagine your client could wave a magic wand to create their perfect solution. What would be on their dream wishlist? Capture those aspirations in detail to better understand their ultimate goals.

Finally, put yourself in their shoes.

EXERCISE 12: Step into your client's mind

Imagine you are the ideal client after purchasing from you. What convinced you to buy? How did it solve your pains? How do you now feel?

Stepping into your client's perspective builds deeper empathy and understanding.

Defining your ideal client and deeply understanding their pains and desires is the foundation for effectively marketing yourself. This knowledge helps craft messages that powerfully resonate with the right people.

It's All About the Language

Leave creativity to artists. One big mistake I see B2B professionals make is trying to be creative with language from their perspective rather than speaking the language of their ideal clients. Do your homework and speak their language.

Doing so will allow your message to resonate with them, gaining their trust by solving their problem. Let their desires be reflected in everything you do, say, and write, from your LinkedIn profile to the messages you send them and the content you create and share.

Imagine you're a business coach, and you want to work with clients who are looking for ways to grow their business and make more money. You plan your approach and your marketing message to attract clients. Which of the following questions will likely get the best response?

1. Are you seeking more abundance and financial freedom?
2. Are you a business owner looking to attract more clients and make more money?

The answer is simple—it's the one that they say to themselves or the people they share their thoughts and problems with. The best way to know the words and phrases your ideal clients use is to:

- Listen to the language used by your current clients
- Listen to the language used when a prospect wants to learn more about what you have to offer
- Listen to the questions asked by your prospects and clients

Notice all three require you to listen, really listen. Being aware of the words and phrases commonly used by your ideal clients is very important, because that is the exact language you want to include in your profile. Take notes each time you are speaking to a prospect or a client, and write down the precise language they use.

Your Why is Your Differentiator

Be clear on your why. In addition to determining who your ideal clients are and what they need, you also need to be clear on who you are, what you stand for, and why you do what you do. While there is probably no one who clarifies this concept as succinctly as Simon Sinek in his TED Talk, "How Great Leaders Inspire Action," I will attempt to explain what it is and why it is so vital to your success.

Your prospects have many options; they will choose you when they can emotionally connect with your message and why you do what you do. If you try to speak to everyone, you will end up speaking to no one. You need to be very clear about who you are trying to attract on LinkedIn and through your social selling efforts. If you fail to do this, you won't get their attention.

Connect with them emotionally, and you will build a relationship. If you can speak and connect with a target audience and build a relationship of trust with them, you will have a loyal group of people who *want* what *you* have to offer.

Remember that regardless of who you sell to, companies or individuals, it is the person who is making the decision that you are building a relationship with. You need to build trust and credibility in the process with that individual. And to do that, they need to know three important things about you:

- You sincerely care
- You understand their specific problem

- You have a solution to *their* problem

The only thing that differentiates you from your competitors is your why! Don't get stuck on what you do or how you do it, but focus rather on the underlying reason why you offer your solution. Simplify this to a few sentences that reflect your motivations to your ideal clients.

Getting to Know Your Ideal Clients on LinkedIn

Recognizing your ideal clients' behaviors and preferences on LinkedIn, and the content they engage with, can greatly improve your social selling strategy. Try the following activities:

- **Mine LinkedIn analytics for valuable observations:** LinkedIn offers a wealth of data about behavior through its built-in analytics. Regularly checking these insights can help you grasp what appeals to your audience, what kind of content they interact with, and when they are most active. For example, LinkedIn post analytics provide data like their job titles, locations, industries, company size, and companies of the people viewing your content. Using this information, you can ensure you are reaching the right demographics and craft content that is more personalized and relevant.
- **Identify engagement patterns and trends:** Knowing how your audience engages is crucial for success on LinkedIn. Pay attention to the posts that get the most likes, comments, and shares. What do these top-performing posts have in common? Is there a specific topic that spurs more engagement? Does a certain format (text, image, video, long-form article) resonate more with your audience? The answers to these questions can guide you in tailoring your content strategy to your ideal clients' preferences.

- **Use LinkedIn's Social Selling Index:** LinkedIn's SSI, discussed in the previous chapter, measures how effectively you're utilizing the platform's features to establish your professional brand, find the right people, engage with insights, and build relationships. Regularly monitoring your SSI score can offer valuable insights into how well you're connecting with your audience, and highlight areas where you could improve.

- **Embrace different approaches:** Finally, it's important to remember that understanding audience behavior is an ongoing process that needs constant experimentation and adaptation. Try various content forms, engage with your audience in different ways, and always be ready to learn and adjust based on the feedback you receive.

Understanding your prospects' behavior and preferences on LinkedIn involves more than just knowing their demographics. It means diving deeper into their interactions, interests, and pain points. By leveraging the platform's features and analytics, you can uncover some valuable insights and customize your social selling strategy for more meaningful and successful interactions.

Defining Your LinkedIn and Social Selling Goals

Before diving into your LinkedIn social selling strategy, it's crucial to first establish your objectives. These goals will serve as the compass for your strategy and action plan. Here are some examples of social selling goals:

- Increasing sales and revenue
- Amplifying brand awareness

- Positioning yourself as a subject matter expert to increase authority
- Generating more leads and prospects
- Building relationships with new prospects
- Nurturing and enhancing relationships with existing clients
- Improving customer service and retention

Create a list of specific objectives you hope to accomplish via LinkedIn and social selling. This list should be precise, guiding you in determining the metrics needed to monitor and measure your success. Some metrics you might consider include:

- SSI score
- 1st-degree connections
- Post impressions
- Appointments booked
- Sales in the pipeline
- New clients acquired
- Revenue generated

EXERCISE: Set Your LinkedIn Goals

Write down three to five specific goals you wish to achieve through LinkedIn and social selling. Make this list as precise as possible, which will help you identify the metrics needed to measure your progress and success toward these goals.

For successful social selling outcomes, it's critical to nurture relationships with prospects and focus on three key elements: understanding your ideal clients, tuning into the language they use, and recognizing the challenges they encounter. Setting clear goals based on this information lays the groundwork for crafting a compelling LinkedIn profile and executing a successful social selling strategy.

Now that you have a deeper understanding of your ideal clients, you're ready to apply this knowledge.

Step 1: Gain Clarity on Your Ideal Client: Start by creating a list of characteristics that define your ideal client by completing all the exercises in this chapter.

Step 2: Set Your LinkedIn Goals: Identify what you would like to achieve on LinkedIn. Once you know what your goals are, you will be able to measure them.

Step 3: Download This Book's Supplemental Resource Pack: To ensure you get the most from this important chapter, I've included all the exercises in a downloadable resource. This resource pack not only includes exercises from this chapter for easy reference, but also features resources from other chapters of the book, offering you a comprehensive guide to mastering social selling on LinkedIn.

Visit **LinkedinUnlockedBook.com** and use the secret word *Bonus* to download your free copy, and start applying these exercises to identify your ideal client effectively and create an emotional connection.

CHAPTER THREE

Transform Your LinkedIn Profile to Attract Clients

Your personal brand functions as a virtual handshake, introducing you to the world. It's not about delivering a sales pitch; instead, it showcases what sets you apart from others. It emphasizes your unique skills, experiences, and values that resonate with potential leads. Think of your LinkedIn profile as a digital version of this handshake—it provides a unique expression of who you are.

A well-crafted LinkedIn profile does more than supplement your resume. When skillfully constructed, it can:

- Attract potential leads and clients, drawing them into your network.
- Present you professionally, highlighting your expertise.
- Demonstrate your knowledge and authority in your field.
- Build trust rapidly with those who view your profile.
- Initiate meaningful conversations with decision-makers.
- Ensure you stand out and are remembered.

In this chapter, I'll cover the essentials of crafting an outstanding LinkedIn profile. I'll guide you through the aspects of appearing professional, engaging with your target audience, and framing your profile as a valuable resource, not just a resume. Follow this advice, and you'll be well on your way to making a strong first impression and building quality, lasting connections.

A Storytelling Business Card for the Digital World

Your LinkedIn profile often serves as the first impression for potential clients, making it vital in your social selling journey. A comprehensive and informative profile not only establishes your credibility but also entices prospects to engage with you.

Never overlook the importance of having a complete LinkedIn profile for achieving success in social selling. According to LinkedIn's State of Sales Report, 50% of buyers avoid professionals with incomplete LinkedIn profiles. Meanwhile, 62% of decision-makers seek informative LinkedIn profiles when contemplating engaging with a sales professional.

A web search of your name is usually the first step for someone wanting to learn more about you. Your LinkedIn profile will almost always appear near the top of these search results, and often will be the first thing they'll click on. Your LinkedIn profile is more often than not the first impression someone will get of you online.

Reframe how you see your LinkedIn profile, viewing it as a useful and informative resource for prospects. It gives them a comprehensive, professional overview of you and can leave a lasting impression—be it positive or negative.

Warmth, Competence, and First Impressions

First impressions matter, especially on LinkedIn, where a quick glance at your profile can form lasting opinions. What are viewers looking for? According to research by Harvard Business School's Amy Cuddy, in collaboration with psychologists Susan and Peter Glick, people typically (often subconsciously) ask two main questions when forming a first impression about someone:

- Can I trust this person?
- Do I respect this person?

These questions underscore two critical qualities: warmth and competence. For a powerful first impression, both attributes are crucial. However, warmth—which in this context means trustworthiness—takes precedence. Establishing trust lays the groundwork for evaluating your skills and knowledge.

Warmth and competence extend beyond simple first impressions. They form the bedrock of human interaction, influencing everything from personal bonds to business collaborations. In the context of LinkedIn, it's paramount to exhibit both trustworthiness and expertise.

People Connect with People

Regardless of your target audience, always remember that people connect with people, not logos, brands, products, or slogans. That's why a warm, authentic, and professional profile is crucial for building trust and demonstrating competence. Avoid sounding overly promotional. Instead, let prospects perceive how you can help them rather than focusing on your sales pitch. Remember, relationships first and selling second. At its core, it should always be about what you can do for them.

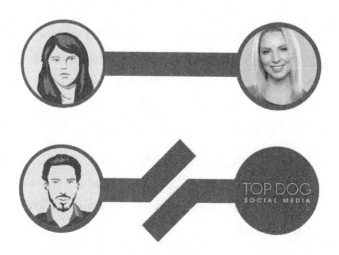

The Power of Mirroring

Within the landscape of lead generation and sales, it's quite common for B2B professionals to stumble when they approach conversations solely from their own perspective, often in an attempt to sound clever. To truly connect, speak your ideal client's language. This means using the terms they would employ when discussing their role, company, industry, challenges, and problems—a technique known as "mirroring."

The language can vary within a single business. For example, communicating with a business owner is going to be different than speaking with a marketing director or sales manager. By tailoring your language to specific roles, you resonate with your audience and demonstrate an understanding of their unique challenges. So make sure to do your homework and speak your prospects' language.

Seven Key Elements to Attract Your Ideal Clients

To make your LinkedIn profile truly magnetic to prospects, consider incorporating these seven key elements. They'll help your profile stand out and connect more effectively with your target audience.

Use the right keywords: The right keywords help people who are looking for your product or service to find you. Use keywords in your profile that are focused on the solutions you deliver. These will capture the attention of viewers of your profile looking for those skills or solutions, and they will help you be found more often in LinkedIn's search results.

Share your "why:" Getting found is only the start. You also need to keep people interested. Sharing your company's "why"—the reason your company exists—can set you apart from your competition and make a deeper connection with your audience.

Show your credibility: Trust is a cornerstone of any good relationship, including business ones. Your profile needs to show you're trustworthy and credible. More on how to do this later in the chapter.

Talk directly to your ideal clients: Your profile should speak directly to the people you most want to reach. Make sure your About and Experience sections clearly highlight who your ideal clients are and how you can help them.

Include a call to action: Guide prospects toward the next step with a clear call to action (CTA). Whether it's inviting them to download a free resource, schedule a consultation, or get in touch via email or phone, a good CTA can help generate leads and facilitate further engagement.

Prove your authority: Your profile should show that you know your stuff. That's where additional resources come in, like articles, whitepapers, or videos that help educate your prospects and provide solutions to their problems.

Stand out from the crowd: Tailor your profile to clearly highlight your unique value proposition, skills, and achievements setting you apart as an industry expert.

Remember, your LinkedIn profile is like your online home for your personal brand. By incorporating these seven key elements, you're well on your way to creating a profile that attracts your ideal clients and helps your business grow. Now let's cover the specific steps to do this.

Steps to Create a Compelling and Credible LinkedIn Profile

Step 1: Craft your profile headline

Your LinkedIn headline is the visitor's first glimpse into your professional world. It sits right next to your name and profile photo, making it a key part of their initial impression. But don't just settle for your job title or throw in some fancy industry jargon. These approaches can feel impersonal or might even confuse your target audience.

Instead, use the 220 characters available in your headline to spark a sense of interest or curiosity. Provide a succinct yet tantalizing taste of your or your company's expertise. You're aiming to inspire visitors to click on your profile and learn more about you.

Here are three time-tested formulas to help you craft a compelling headline. Pick the one that best aligns with your goals, target audience, and unique flavor of your personal brand:

- **Social proof:** Clients will always gravitate towards people/businesses who clearly understand their industry and have experience working with individuals or companies like theirs. You can create credibility by mentioning successes with similar clients. For example: "Helped over 100 digital marketing agencies increase revenue by 27% on average."
- **Intrigue:** Instead of trying to sell yourself outright, craft a headline that inspires curiosity. For example: "In the last ten months I helped 44 corporate employees quit their job and create their dream life."
- **Interest:** Want to provoke interest? Combine a brief overview of what you do with some social proof/results. For example:

"Marketing Strategist for Local San Diego Businesses | Over $15M in Business Growth Delivered."

As an example, I focus on social proof in my own LinkedIn headline by noting that I'm the author of several books:

Melonie Dodaro

Author of LinkedIn Unlocked [Second Edition]; Navigating LinkedIn for Sales; and Supercharged: Ignite Your Sales and Marketing with Artificial Intelligence

---

Remember, your headline is not just your job title and company name—it's your invitation to prospects to explore more about you professionally and how you can help them. Make it count!

Step 2: Display a professional headshot

Your profile picture plays a huge part in the first impression you make on prospects. It's a key part of your online identity and personal brand. A professional headshot can be the difference between someone deciding to explore your profile further or simply passing you by.

Your profile picture should present you as approachable and professional. You want to choose an image that is recognizably you, shows you dressed professionally, and features you smiling at the camera against a clean, neutral backdrop.

Here are some tips to guide you when choosing or taking your profile picture:

- Use a current photo. You want people to recognize you from your picture.
- Make sure your face takes up at least 60% of the frame. This allows viewers to clearly see your features.

- Flash a genuine smile. Showing some teeth often appears warmer and inviting.
- Dress in professional clothing that fits with your role and industry.
- Choose a simple, uncluttered background.
- Look directly at the camera. This can create a feeling of direct engagement with the viewer. Keep the focus on you. Avoid including other people in your profile picture.
- Skip the filters. They can sometimes come off as unprofessional.

A strong, professional profile photo can serve as an inviting entry point to your LinkedIn profile. It's a small but powerful step in building your online presence and attracting prospects.

Step 3: Set your profile photo to public

LinkedIn, distinct from other social platforms, allows you to adjust the visibility of your profile photo. To maximize your outreach and the impact of your profile, it's crucial to make your photo visible to everyone.

You might have noticed during a LinkedIn search that some users' profile pictures are missing, leaving a blank space next to their names and headlines. While some of these individuals may not have uploaded a profile photo, others have restricted their photo's visibility. Sometimes, LinkedIn may default your profile photo visibility to "Your Network" only, but this setting isn't ideal for you. Having a blank avatar can be likened to introducing yourself to a room full of potential clients while wearing a paper bag over your head—it's not the impression you want to make!

Follow these steps to set your profile photo visibility to "Public:"

1. Navigate to your LinkedIn profile page.
2. Click on the "Edit public profile & URL" link in the top right-hand corner.

3. This action opens a new page, enabling you to adjust your profile visibility settings.

4. On the right-hand side of the screen, under "Edit Visibility," locate the "Profile Photo" option.

5. Change the visibility to "Public."

6. Your changes will save automatically. Your LinkedIn profile photo is now visible to anyone who finds you via LinkedIn or other search engines.

Always remember: your goal is to present a personal, approachable image to potential clients. They want to see who they're engaging with, and a friendly, professional profile picture can set the tone for future business relationships.

Step 4: Add a cover photo

Your cover photo plays a significant role on your LinkedIn profile, standing out prominently displayed behind your profile picture. This area is a unique opportunity to draw in prospects with an intriguing and professional image that communicates who you are and what you provide. Some examples include:

- **A professionally constructed graphic:** Embodying your company's essence or your profession.

- **A compilation of images:** Showcasing you in action, whether helping clients or speaking at events.

- **Attention-grabbing elements:** An impactful headline along with your company logo.

- **Your mission or vision statement:** Conveying your core values and purpose.

- **A timeline of milestones:** Highlighting key moments or achievements in your career or company's history.

- **Testimonials or endorsements:** A powerful quote from a client or industry leader to establish credibility.
- **An inspirational quote:** Choose one that encapsulates your work ethic, philosophy, or industry insight.
- **Dynamic elements:** Images or graphs demonstrating your growth, capabilities, or industry metrics.
- **Geographic emphasis:** If localized expertise is your strength, feature relevant landmarks or geography.
- **A call to action (CTA):** An invitation for viewers to connect, explore a project, or visit your website.

As with your profile photo, your cover photo should emphasize the professionalism and consistency of your personal brand. It can also serve as an engaging conversation starter.

Here's an example of a cover photo I have used showcasing my books. While I do reference them in my headline, a picture truly speaks a thousand words.

While your cover photo provides a visual statement of your personal brand, it's also an ideal space to give viewers a quick understanding of who you are, the company you represent, and what you bring to the table.

To make sure your cover image fits perfectly on your LinkedIn profile, use an image that meets the correct dimensions. LinkedIn occasionally updates the size requirements for the cover photo, so it's a good idea to check the current standards before you create your image. If your image size is smaller than the minimum requirements, your cover photo might appear blurred or pixelated. Ensure the image file size doesn't exceed 8MB and is in a JPG or PNG format. Also keep in mind that one side of your cover photo will be cut off by your profile photo, so leave room for that as I have in the example I shared above.

Step 5: Specify your location

Including your current location in your LinkedIn profile is especially important if you are targeting a specific geographic region. By specifying your location, you enhance your visibility in searches, increasing the likelihood of being found by up to 23 times, according to research from LinkedIn. This geographic detail can also create a sense of relatability, serving as a touchpoint of relatedness when establishing connections and nurturing relationships with prospects.

Step 6: Include your contact information

On LinkedIn, your contact information section displays both your profile URL and the email address linked with your account. If you've used a personal email but wish to showcase a professional one, simply add a second email. You can then set your preferred email as the primary one, which will then be the one displayed within your "contact info" section. LinkedIn also allows you to list your website and phone number.

It's important to note that only your 1st-degree connections can view your email and phone number in the contact section. If you'd like a broader audience to see them, consider adding them to your "About" or "Experience" sections.

Step 7: Customize your LinkedIn public profile URL

LinkedIn automatically generates a profile URL for you, combining your first and last names with random numbers and symbols. However, creating a customized URL that is easy to remember can help potential clients find you quickly. You should select a URL that is simple and includes your name or a variation of it.

To modify your profile URL, click on "Edit public profile & URL" in the top right corner of your profile. Then, click on the edit icon next to your current URL, and edit the last part of the URL to include your name. Make sure your URL includes only letters and numbers, devoid of any spaces, symbols, or special characters. After adjusting the URL, hit the "Save" button.

Keep in mind that you can alter your URL only five times within a six-month span, so choose one you are satisfied with for the long-term. To streamline the process for prospects to find you, consider integrating your personalized profile URL in your email signature and other marketing channels.

Melonie Dodaro

Contact Info

 ## Your Profile
linkedin.com/in/meloniedodaro

Step 8: Assist others in pronouncing your name correctly

Correctly pronouncing a person's name holds significant importance when initiating any professional relationship. To facilitate this, LinkedIn has a feature that allows you to record the pronunciation of your name and add it to your profile. This is especially useful if your name has a unique pronunciation that's not evident from its spelling.

To add this feature, you'll need to use the LinkedIn mobile app, which is available on iOS and Android. Follow these steps:

1. Open the LinkedIn app and tap on your profile picture to go to your profile.
2. Tap on the "Record name pronunciation" button, located below your profile picture.
3. Follow the on-screen instructions to record and review your name pronunciation.
4. Once you're satisfied with the recording, tap "Save."

Now, viewers of your profile can hear the correct pronunciation of your name, helping pave the way for smoother and more respectful interactions.

Importantly, always take the time to listen to name pronunciations on the profiles of your prospects if they have this feature enabled. Understanding and correctly pronouncing a prospect's name is a basic yet crucial aspect of building rapport. Respecting this small detail can set the tone for your business relationship and make your interactions more personal and meaningful.

Step 9: Add gender pronouns (optional)

Promoting a culture of respect, inclusion, and diversity is important to some individuals and their organizations. One way of demonstrating this is by adding your gender pronouns (such as she/her, he/him, they/them, or a custom option) to your LinkedIn profile.

This practice has gained significant traction to avoid assumptions and miscommunication about individuals' gender identities. By sharing your pronouns, you're signaling to prospects and colleagues that you respect and affirm people's identities. This act can go a long way in developing positive relationships and contributing to an inclusive professional environment.

To add your gender pronouns, follow these steps:

1. Click on "Me" on your LinkedIn homepage.
2. Select "View profile."
3. Click on the "Add profile section" button.
4. Under the "Intro" section, select "Pronouns."
5. In the pop-up window, enter your preferred pronouns.
6. Click on "Save" to apply the changes to your profile.

Besides using your pronouns, ensure you respect and use the appropriate pronouns for your contacts, clients, and prospects if they've added them to their profiles. Just as with the name pronunciation feature, this small attention to detail can contribute greatly to building rapport.

Step 10: Personalize your About section

The "About" section is the linchpin of your LinkedIn profile. It's your chance to let prospects know more about you, beyond your professional history. This section should not merely replicate your resume or professional bio; instead, it should speak to your ideal client. Avoid sales language in this section and instead portray yourself as a valuable resource, equipped to solve their issues and drive substantial results.

Here are some strategic tips to create a compelling, client-centric About section:

- **Adopt a first-person voice**: Keep the tone conversational and relatable, creating a more personal connection.
- **Showcase your qualifications**: Feature your skills, experience, and education to instill credibility and trust in your target market. Use specific examples to show how your expertise can benefit prospects.
- **Address your ideal clients**: Speak directly to your ideal clients' pain points, offering your unique solutions. Make them feel seen and understood.
- **Utilize space efficiently**: Use the given 2,600 characters wisely, ensuring each word contributes value.

Let's delve deeper into the critical elements that should be conveyed in your About section.

Showcase credibility: Narrate your professional history, focusing on pertinent experiences and achievements. Introduce yourself and detail your expertise and successes. Also, address key questions prospects might have, such as:

- Who are you?
- What do you do?
- Who are your typical clients?
- How do you deliver results?
- Why do you do what you do?
- Why should they trust you?

Strengthen your credibility with social proof, such as accolades, published works, industry recognition, and testimonials.

Identify your ideal clients: Clearly defining your ideal clients helps them recognize themselves in your narrative. Describe the types of clients you cater to and address their specific problems. Structure your client descriptions this way:

- Mention your ideal client role
- Describe that person's problem or challenge
- Describe how your solution addresses that problem
- Mention the benefits of your solution

For example:

> **CONSULTANTS AND SERVICE PROVIDERS:** Are you facing challenges in attracting clients who recognize the value of your expertise and are ready to invest in quality? LinkedIn is a goldmine of high-caliber leads. I specialize in strategies that make you irresistible to premium clients on LinkedIn, ensuring they not only want to work with you but can also afford your top-tier services.

Have a clear call to action: Your CTA should direct prospects to their next steps, be it a phone call, an email, or a LinkedIn message. A good CTA should be:

- Transparent and concise: Avoid ambiguity.
- Action-driven: Use proactive verbs.
- Value-oriented: Highlight the benefit of action.
- Urgent: Prompt immediate action with timely incentives.
- Instructional: Clearly guide prospects on how to proceed.

Your CTA concludes your profile, gently prompting prospects to initiate contact. Invest time in creating a persuasive CTA that effectively nudges your prospects toward the desired action.

Step 11: Enable the Featured section

The Featured section on LinkedIn is more than just a space to share educational materials. It serves as your personal exhibit hall to spotlight your recent achievements, work samples, and upcoming events. By showcasing these, you affirm your expertise and establish credibility with potential clients.

Select from a range of options for your Featured content. These could be links to external resources, media uploads, or even your most popular LinkedIn posts.

Incorporating videos into your profile can help establish a more personal connection with your audience. Consider using videos to showcase your products/services, expertise, or client testimonials. Similarly, PDFs can be an effective way to share educational resources such as articles and white papers, as well as marketing materials.

Remember, the content you highlight should resonate with your ideal clients and enhance your personal brand. Regular updates to your Featured section will keep your profile fresh and appealing, piquing the interest of prospects.

Step 12: Complete your Experience section

The Experience section is where you can display your current and past roles and achievements, with up to 2,000 characters available for a comprehensive description of each position. Similar to your About section, your description should focus on your company's credibility and how it can help prospects and clients.

Current work experience

Start by defining your company and its standout characteristics. This could cover aspects such as unique selling points, awards, and accomplishments. If you have a website, you may already have some of this written on your About page.

Next, detail the products or services you offer and the benefits they provide. Tailor your descriptions to your ideal client, emphasizing how your solution can address their specific needs and problems.

Consider enhancing social proof by listing notable current or previous clients. If you've collaborated with recognizable names, include them. If your clients aren't well-known, you could instead mention the industries or professions you cater to, like digital marketing agencies, coaches, consultants, and speakers.

Powerful testimonials from clients can be highly persuasive. Sharing one or two short testimonials in your description can deepen the trust prospects have in your ability to deliver results.

Finally, conclude your description with another call to action. This CTA could echo the one in your About section or be a slightly different variant. Ensure you make it clear what action you'd like the viewer to take next, inspiring them to engage with you.

Title of your current work experience

When inputting your title for your current work experience on LinkedIn, it is beneficial to avoid anything sales-related. If you are in a sales role, instead of choosing titles such as Account Manager, think about using language that describes your area of expertise. For example, if your role was in business development for a marketing agency, instead of displaying Business Development in your title, you could write Digital Marketing Specialist. Adopting this approach can help to avert prospects from rejecting your connection request due to concerns of an immediate sales pitch.

Add multimedia to your current work experience

Adding multimedia to your current work experience can enhance its impact on your LinkedIn profile. To do this, navigate to your current role under the Experience section and click the edit pencil. Once that position opens, scroll down to the "Media" section and click on the "+ Add media" icon. This allows you to upload or link to multimedia content that is relevant to your current experience.

Consider including items such as presentations, project showcases, video testimonials, or published works that you've contributed to. This acts as a dynamic portfolio, providing prospects with a glimpse of your expertise and how you help clients like them. Ensure the multimedia content you include is professionally appropriate and relevant to your current position.

Past experience

While your past experience doesn't require as much detail as your current role, it's beneficial to include a succinct overview of each prior position to provide a comprehensive view of your professional history. Doing so conveys more trust and provides a more robust LinkedIn profile.

In each past role, focus on key achievements or milestones that illustrate your skill set and proficiency. Even if a past role doesn't align directly with your present industry, emphasize any transferable skills that could be attractive to prospects.

Step 13: Fill out your Skills section

The Skills section is crucial to showcasing your abilities relevant to your current and past experience. This helps prospects understand both your expertise and the value you could bring to their organization. If you offer a particular service or solution, ensure your profile reflects these skills.

LinkedIn lets your connections endorse your skills, which adds to your social proof.

To ensure your most relevant skills are immediately visible, LinkedIn permits you to arrange your skills, placing the top three at the forefront. Additionally, you can link specific skills to your experience and education sections, providing a richer context and demonstrating your expertise and proficiency in these areas.

Step 14: Complete your Education section

Your Education section highlights degrees or certifications, fields of study, and activities. It also allows you to include a brief description for each. This can initiate conversations with prospects who attended the same school or majored in a similar field.

Tapping into your alma mater's network can uncover potential connections through the "Network with Alumni" feature. If you're engaged in ongoing education, such as a certification or degree program, include this in your Education section with the anticipated completion date. This can demonstrate your commitment to continuous learning and professional growth.

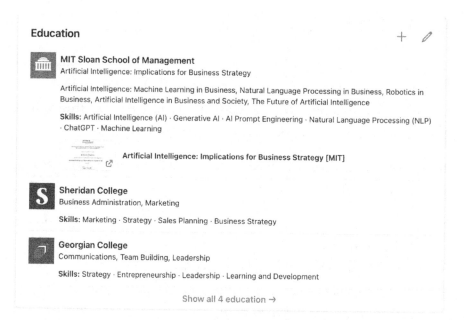

Education   +   ✎

MIT Sloan School of Management
Artificial Intelligence: Implications for Business Strategy

Artificial Intelligence: Machine Learning in Business, Natural Language Processing in Business, Robotics in Business, Artificial Intelligence in Business and Society, The Future of Artificial Intelligence

Skills: Artificial Intelligence (AI) · Generative AI · AI Prompt Engineering · Natural Language Processing (NLP) · ChatGPT · Machine Learning

Artificial Intelligence: Implications for Business Strategy [MIT]

Sheridan College
Business Administration, Marketing

Skills: Marketing · Strategy · Sales Planning · Business Strategy

Georgian College
Communications, Team Building, Leadership

Skills: Strategy · Entrepreneurship · Leadership · Learning and Development

Show all 4 education →

Step 15: Add the Volunteer experience section if relevant

The Volunteer experience section is an excellent platform to highlight your community involvement and charitable endeavors. Including this section can give prospects insight into your personal values, interests, and supported causes.

When listing your volunteer experience, include the organization's name, your role, the volunteering duration, and a brief description of your duties and achievements.

Multimedia can enhance the presentation of your volunteer work even further. You can incorporate photos or videos from volunteer events you've attended, or links to articles or blog posts you authored.

To add the Volunteer experience section to your profile, select the "Add profile section" button to the right of your name and headline at the top of your profile. Look for "Volunteer experience" under the "Additional" section.

Step 16: Add the Accomplishments section if relevant

The Accomplishments section serves as a platform to professionally and comprehensively showcase your career highlights. It helps establish your credibility and authority, allowing prospects to know, like, and trust you. It can also provide commonalities to connect with prospects.

If you wish to integrate your various accomplishments, you'll need to manually add them, similarly to your volunteer experience. The Accomplishments section comprises various categories:

- **Publications:** Listing your published works can increase the likelihood of being found by seven times.
- **Certifications:** Noting a certification can boost profile views by five times, according to LinkedIn.
- **Courses:** Include relevant coursework from your past or continuing education.
- **Projects:** Detail compelling projects to illustrate your experience.
- **Honors & Awards:** Share any awards, accolades, or recognitions you've received.
- **Patents:** Highlight your innovation and expertise.
- **Test Scores:** If you performed exceptionally well on a well-known standardized exam, especially if you are a recent graduate, it can be beneficial to list the test score.
- **Languages:** Exhibit your language proficiency to align with global opportunities.
- **Organizations:** Display your participation in various organizations that matter to you.

It's important to only incorporate categories relevant to your career. Each element should enhance your credibility or offer a potential point of similarity with your prospects.

Step 17: Follow others to showcase your Interests section

The Interests section on your LinkedIn profile is a space that's often undervalued but can be quite beneficial. This section displays the influencers, companies, and schools you follow. By carefully selecting the interests you showcase, you can provide prospects with an insight into your priorities and establish commonalities.

Influencers: Follow thought leaders within your industry or related sectors, along with the leadership team of your own company. This reflects your engagement with key voices in your field and your commitment to continuous learning.

Companies: Start by following your own company page on LinkedIn, and follow the company pages of your top prospects. This approach can help you stay informed on the latest news and developments from these companies, proving useful in future discussions with prospects.

Schools: Be sure to follow the institutions you've attended. This not only highlights your academic background but can also create connections with fellow alumni in your network.

Step 18: Complete your Recommendations section

Getting recommendations is one of the most compelling ways to display social proof of your expertise. When people decide with whom to conduct business, others' decisions often influence them. The more recommendations you have, the better, and the quality of those recommendations is important as well. Aim to secure 5 to 10 recommendations from credible individuals who can genuinely attest to your character and professional competency.

Recommendations can come from colleagues and employers, but particularly impactful are those from your clients. These recommendations can specifically address your skills and contributions in resolving their challenges, which will be compelling for potential clients.

Getting LinkedIn recommendations

Securing recommendations can be straightforward. Timing is key; ask for a recommendation when the person's positive experience with you is still fresh. For example, if you receive praise via email or private message, express your gratitude, then inquire if they would be comfortable converting that into a LinkedIn recommendation.

After reading my last book, a reader sent me private message on LinkedIn sharing her success story. I appreciated her feedback and replied, "Thank you for sharing this with me; it would make an excellent LinkedIn recommendation. Would you be open to writing one for me?"

Another strategy is to request a recommendation from a colleague with whom you've closely collaborated and who is transitioning to a new role at a different company. When suitable, you can reciprocate by recommending them as well.

Also, consider reaching out to past coworkers for recommendations. Be sure to articulate why you're asking for a recommendation and personalize your message. It can be as straightforward as, "I recently read a book on LinkedIn and have been updating my profile. The next step is to request some recommendations. Would you consider writing one for me about the project we collaborated on? I'd be very grateful."

A comprehensive and professional profile, enhanced by recommendations, offers compelling social proof, significantly enhancing your personal brand and social selling efforts.

A Consistent Brand Beyond LinkedIn

Maintaining a consistent brand across all your social media profiles, including LinkedIn, is crucial in establishing trust and building relationships with potential clients. When expanding your social selling strategy to other channels, it's advisable to use the same profile picture and social handle as you do on LinkedIn, making it easier for people to recognize you across different platforms.

Email Signature

Your email signature is often the first impression of you beyond LinkedIn. It's crucial to maintain consistency between your LinkedIn branding and your email signature. Include a link to your LinkedIn profile and consider adding your profile picture as well to strengthen recognition.

Online Sales Presentations/Webinars

If you offer presentations or webinars, ensure the visual elements and tone align with your LinkedIn branding. This creates a cohesive image and can build credibility with prospects.

Events and Networking

When attending events or networking sessions, consider integrating elements from your LinkedIn profile. If you have a custom URL for your LinkedIn profile, share it when relevant.

LINKEDIN PROFILE CHECKLIST

☐ Does your profile's name field only contain your name, without any special characters, icons, or emojis?

☐ Have you updated your headline?

☐ Do you have a professional profile photo with a friendly smile?

☐ Have you added a custom cover image?

☐ Have you secured a vanity URL for your LinkedIn profile, replacing the default one that has a string of numbers?

☐ Did you add your website to your profile?

☐ Did you complete your About section sharing your expertise and speaking directly to your ideal clients?

☐ Did you incorporate multimedia elements like videos, presentations, and PDFs into the Featured section?

☐ Have you described your current experience and shared information about your company, services, and target market?

☐ Have you updated your title/position to one that isn't sales related?

☐ Have you added your past work experience?

☐ Have you updated your Education section?

☐ Did you include volunteer activities, if applicable?

☐ Have you listed your skills in the Skills section?

☐ Have you added any relevant accomplishments like publications, certifications, projects, and awards?

☐ Did you curate your Interests section by following relevant influencers, companies, and institutions?

☐ Have you requested and received recommendations from clients, colleagues, and employers?

Use this checklist as a guide to ensure your LinkedIn profile is polished and ready to attract your ideal clients. And remember, this checklist is not a one-time task. It's a good practice to periodically review your LinkedIn profile and update it as necessary to keep it relevant and impactful.

Your LinkedIn profile is an essential tool in your social selling toolkit. It's crucial to make your profile as strong as possible to create a good first impression and build trust with prospects.

Step 1: Define Your Professional Brand: Think about how you want to portray yourself professionally. What are the key strengths, skills, and values you wish to emphasize? Write these down, as they will form the core of your personal brand.

Step 2: Update Profile Essentials: Begin with updating your headline, profile photo, and About section, then customizing your LinkedIn URL. Make sure these elements are compelling, professional, and client-centric.

Step 3: Highlight Your Experience: Add your employment history to the Experience section, highlighting how you've addressed the needs and challenges of your clients in your current company and past roles.

Step 4: Showcase Education, Volunteer Experience, and Accomplishments: Update your Education and Volunteer sections if applicable. Consider adding the Accomplishments section to showcase your skills and achievements if relevant.

Step 5: Request Recommendations: Seek recommendations from colleagues, former employers, and clients. Their recommendation can enhance your credibility and provide valuable social proof.

In summary, a compelling LinkedIn profile is key to establishing trust, showcasing your expertise, and building relationships with prospects. Follow the steps outlined in this chapter, and you will find that decision-makers will be much more receptive to your connection requests.

CHAPTER FOUR

Compare LinkedIn Subscriptions for Full Potential

LinkedIn has become an essential platform for professionals, businesses, and brands looking to network, recruit talent, grow professionally, and generate leads. However, not all LinkedIn subscriptions are created equal. LinkedIn offers several subscription tiers, both free and paid, each with their own set of features and capabilities.

Deciding which LinkedIn subscription is right for you or your business can be confusing. Should you stick with the basic free version or invest in a paid subscription? Do you need a Premium Business or Sales Navigator plan to achieve your goals on LinkedIn?

The needs and goals of each person using LinkedIn can vary greatly. An entrepreneur just starting out may find the free version fully sufficient, while a sales or marketing professional looking for new leads might require the advanced features of Sales Navigator.

In this chapter, I'll compare the different subscription tiers on LinkedIn— Free, Premium Business, and Sales Navigator. I'll outline the key differences, benefits, and limitations of each plan. You'll learn which features provide the most value depending on how you use LinkedIn.

Whether you want to boost your personal brand, grow a large network, or generate more B2B leads, this chapter will help you decide which LinkedIn subscription is best for you. Let's dive in and unlock the full potential of LinkedIn for your goals.

Free LinkedIn Subscription

Despite its clear limitations, there's a lot to like about LinkedIn's free account. With the free LinkedIn membership, you can:

- Build your professional brand by customizing your profile sections, adding multimedia, and showcasing your expertise, accomplishments, and skills.
- Build and engage with a large, trusted professional network by connecting with colleagues, partners, classmates, clients, and more.
- Find and reconnect with former coworkers, classmates, and business contacts through LinkedIn's powerful search algorithms for finding people from your past professional life.
- Showcase expertise and credibility by receiving recommendations and endorsements for your skills.
- Search for and view profiles of other LinkedIn members to research contacts, competitors, partners, prospects, and more.
- Share relevant posts and articles to build your visibility and establish yourself as an industry authority.
- Send and receive messages from your 1st-degree connections, allowing you to build stronger relationships with your network.
- Join relevant groups to engage in discussions. There are millions of groups on LinkedIn, although most have lost popularity and active participation in recent years.

However, LinkedIn does impose "commercial use limits" on free accounts regarding searches. You can only perform a limited number of searches each month before your results get capped. Activities like searching profiles and looking at "People Also Viewed" suggestions count towards these limits.

Many features once available in the free membership have been removed as well, like seeing who viewed your profile (limited to only the last five with a free account).

The majority of LinkedIn users find a free account to be sufficient; however, many looking to fully unlock LinkedIn's sales and marketing potential choose to upgrade to paid subscriptions. Reasons include:

- Removing search limits so you don't lose access partway through the month.
- Accomplishing more in less time with advanced features like expanded search filters.
- Unlocking profile traffic data to see who may be interested in connecting.
- Messaging decision makers outside your network with InMail credits.

Even with limitations, LinkedIn is still highly valuable for professionals to find and connect with the right people and build a strong personal brand.

Paid LinkedIn Subscriptions

While LinkedIn's free version provides ample value, many professionals and businesses choose to upgrade to paid subscriptions to unlock more advanced capabilities.

LinkedIn offers several paid membership tiers depending on your needs, including:

- **Premium Career**: Ideal for job seekers looking to showcase their experience, skills, and interests to potential employers. Provides tools to find the right jobs and stand out with hiring managers.
- **Premium Business**: Designed for business, sales, and marketing professionals to boost their brand, connect with prospects, and generate leads.

- **Sales Navigator**: LinkedIn's flagship sales solution, providing advanced search, saved lead lists, alerts, and other tools to find ideal prospects and manage relationships.
- **Recruiter Lite**: Enables individual recruiters to source, contact, and manage talent with recruiter-specific tools and InMail messaging.

The chart below comes directly from LinkedIn and compares the Premium Career, Premium Business, Sales Navigator Core, and Recruiter Lite plans to see which may be the best for you.

LinkedIn Paid Subscription Options	Premium Career	Premium Business	Sales Navigator Core	Recruiter Lite
Private Browsing	✓	✓	✓	✓
Applicant Insights	✓	✓	✓	✓
Direct messaging	✓	✓	✓	✓
Who Viewed Your Profile	✓	✓	✓	
Who's viewed your profile insights	90 days	365 days	90 days	90 days
Unlimited access to LinkedIn Learning	✓	✓	✓	✓
Unlimited people browsing		✓	✓	✓
Business Insights		✓	✓	✓
Advanced Search			✓	✓
Standalone sales interface			✓	
Custom lead and account lists			✓	

Lead recommendations and saved leads			✓	
Real-time updates and alerts			✓	
Recruiting-specific design				✓
Automatic candidate tracking				✓
Integrated hiring				✓
Smart Suggestions				✓
InMail credits	5	15	50	30

Note: While the information presented in the chart accurately represents the general access periods for profile views associated with different LinkedIn subscription levels, it's important to mention that my personal experience with Sales Navigator Core has revealed an extended feature. Sales Navigator Core activates LinkedIn Premium, and I've been able to select profile views for the last 365 days, surpassing the standard 90-day access period that LinkedIn states is available. It's worth considering that such features may not be explicitly detailed in the information LinkedIn provides, and that subscription offerings and features may evolve over time.

In this next section, I'll take a deeper look at the key differences between LinkedIn's paid subscription levels. I'll focus primarily on Premium Business and Sales Navigator, the two subscriptions most relevant for leveraging LinkedIn for sales, marketing, and business development.

LinkedIn Premium Business Subscription

If you feel limited by your free LinkedIn account, you might want to consider LinkedIn Premium Business. Here is a list of tools and features you can access with your LinkedIn Premium Business subscription to help you decide if it is right for you:

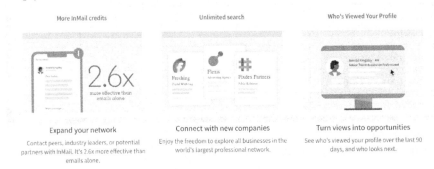

More InMail credits	Unlimited search	Who's Viewed Your Profile

Expand your network	**Connect with new companies**	**Turn views into opportunities**
Contact peers, industry leaders, or potential partners with InMail. It's 2.6x more effective than emails alone.	Enjoy the freedom to explore all businesses in the world's largest professional network.	See who's viewed your profile over the last 90 days, and who looks next.

InMail

If you want to send a message to someone you're not connected to (and with whom you don't share a group), you must send them an *InMail*. InMails can be useful when you want to reach out to a prospect before you send them a connection request, or if they haven't accepted your connection request. This is only possible with a paid subscription. You're given a certain number of InMails every month based on your subscription level, with an opportunity to purchase more.

Unlimited Search

With unlimited people browsing, you don't have to worry about the commercial use limits put on free accounts. This means you won't lose access to search results before the month ends, which would negatively affect your lead generation searches. Activities that LinkedIn counts towards the commercial use limits include:

- Searching for LinkedIn profiles on LinkedIn.com or the mobile app
- Browsing LinkedIn profiles using the "People Also Viewed" section located on the right rail of a profile

These activities do not count toward the limit:

- Searching profiles by name using the search box located at the top of every page on LinkedIn.com
- Browsing your 1st-degree connections from the Connections page within "My Network"
- Searching for jobs on the Jobs page

Who's Viewed Your Profile

This feature is one of LinkedIn's most popular, because it reveals the types of people and companies your profile and skillset is attracting, often uncovering high-quality potential leads. This section lists all the people who have viewed your profile (you can see only the last five people with a free account).

LinkedIn provides you with some additional filters in the "Who's viewed your profile" section as well, including:

- Company (see if there is a trend of people from specific companies viewing your profile)
- Industry (discover what industries your viewers are in)
- Location (see the most common geographical locations of your viewers)

And if you click on "All filters" you will also be able to see:

- Date range (past 14 days, 28 days, 90 days, 365 days)
- Interesting viewers*

*LinkedIn defines "Interesting viewers" in its analytics as notable profile viewers, such as senior leaders in your industry, recruiters, and other individuals who can further your career. Turning on the "Interesting viewers" feature in LinkedIn's analytics will show you these notable profile viewers.

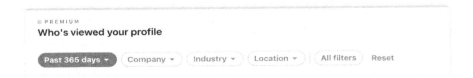

LinkedIn Learning

Your monthly subscription gives you access to LinkedIn Learning, which can be found within LinkedIn itself. In the Learning Center, you will find a wide variety of courses and content under three central themes: business, creative, and technology.

Whether you are just looking to brush up on your knowledge of a particular topic or learn something new, this is an excellent professional resource included with all paid LinkedIn subscriptions.

The Limitations of a LinkedIn Premium Subscription

While the LinkedIn Premium subscription offers additional features beyond the free account, this membership has limitations for people who are looking to use LinkedIn for social selling.

One benefit LinkedIn claims for a Premium Business membership is the InMail credits provided. While InMail allows you to send messages to LinkedIn users who aren't in your network, I find that InMails tend to underperform compared to standard LinkedIn messages. InMails have open rates of only around 20-25% compared to over 50% for regular messages, likely because they appear more promotional in a user's inbox. As a result, response rates to InMails are lower as well. Unless you need to message non-connections, standard LinkedIn messages tend to drive better engagement.

Another potential drawback of the LinkedIn Premium Business subscription for those wanting to focus on lead generation is the lack of advanced search and targeting filters. Premium's limited search capabilities impede efficient lead generation. Without advanced filters, you can't target prospects based on attributes like seniority, years at company, job function, company size, or other crucial criteria. Premium also lacks the ability to save complex searches or get daily alerts when new matches are made, which Sales Navigator enables. This means more manual effort is required to surface ideal new prospects.

Premium Business does not provide lead recommendations or tracking features like Sales Navigator offers. Sales Navigator systematically recommends the most relevant prospects and accounts for you to prioritize based on your search criteria. It also allows you to "follow" leads to receive real-time alerts when they make changes at their company or share posts. This level of targeting and automation is not possible with Premium.

Finally, Premium lacks the integrated sales workflow features and UI of Sales Navigator. Sales Navigator provides a streamlined experience tailored for sales, with customized lead lists, notes and reminders on leads, and much more. Premium Business has a more generalized experience that caters to a wider audience. Those focused heavily on social selling will likely find Sales Navigator's sales-centric tools more efficient.

LinkedIn Sales Navigator

For those dedicated to lead generation and sales prospecting, Sales Navigator is LinkedIn's premier subscription. In comparison to the other subscriptions, Sales Navigator stands out for its advanced search capabilities. These allow you to accurately identify and target your ideal clients based on a variety of criteria that go way beyond just job function, seniority, company size, and geographical location.

Another unique feature of Sales Navigator is the ability to save and track leads and accounts. With this, you can monitor the activity of potential leads and companies, allowing you to reach out at the optimal moment or stay up to date with any significant changes.

Sales Navigator has three versions tailored to different needs:

- **Sales Navigator Core** provides robust tools for individual social sellers and sales professionals.
- **Sales Navigator Advanced** enables team collaboration capabilities like TeamLink to connect sales teams.
- **Sales Navigator Advanced Plus** offers enterprise-level integration, CRM synchronization, and advanced analytics.

Here is a chart summarizing the key differences between the three Sales Navigator plans:

SALES NAVIGATOR FEATURES AND PLANS	CORE	ADVANCED	ADVANCED PLUS
Access to LinkedIn subscriptions *Job seeker, LinkedIn Learning access*	✓		
Extended network access *Unlimited search, Saved searches, Who's viewed your profile in the past 90 days*	✓	✓	✓
Reach out *InMail*	✓	✓	✓
Find the right people *Advanced search, sales spotlights*	✓	✓	✓
Prioritize and qualify *Lead and account recommendations, sales preferences*	✓	✓	✓
Integrate with your sales tools *SNAP, Outlook web integration, Sales Navigator mobile app (SNAP for Advanced and Advanced Plus only)*	✓	✓	✓

Feature			
Keep track of people and companies *Saved leads/accounts, Custom lists, Alerts, Notes (Buyer Interest alerts for Advanced and Advanced Plus only)*	✓	✓	✓
Engage with your prospects and customers using your team's network *TeamLink, TeamLink Extend*		✓	✓
Advanced outreach—package content and track engagement *Smart Links*		✓	✓
Administrative tools/reporting *Usage Reporting, Account Center*		✓	✓
Centralized billing for contracts sold through LinkedIn corporate sales *Volume and multi-year discounts, invoicing, dedicated relationship manager*		✓	✓
Enterprise tools *SSO, Employee Data Integration*		✓	✓
CRM Sync *Auto-Save, Activity Writeback, & ROI Reporting for Salesforce and Microsoft Dynamics 365 Sales*			✓
Advanced CRM integrations *Data Validation & Contact Creation for Salesforce and Microsoft Dynamics 365*			✓

Let me share just some of what makes Sales Navigator powerful for finding, connecting, and staying engaged with your ideal clients.

Sales Navigator Advanced Search

Sales Navigator Advanced Search provides additional filters for finding leads and accounts. The search filters are divided into two categories: People Search Filters (Leads) and Company Search Filters (Accounts).

The Sales Navigator Advanced Search filters include:

Company

- Company headcount
- Current company
- Past company
- Company type
- Company headquarters

Role

- Current job title
- Past job title
- Function
- Seniority level
- Years in current company
- Years in current position

Spotlights

- Changed jobs in last 90 days
- Mentioned in news in last 30 days
- Posted on LinkedIn in last 30 days
- Following your company
- Have shared experiences with you
- With TeamLink intro

- With TeamLink intro through your executives
- Past customer (only with Advanced Plus with CRM integration)
- Past colleague

Posted Content

- Keywords in article

Personal

- Connection
- Geography
- Industry
- Years of experience
- Connections of
- Groups
- First Name
- Last Name
- Profile language
- TeamLink connections of
- School

Workflow

- Lead lists
- People in CRM
- Persona
- Account lists
- People you interacted with
- Saved leads and accounts

Lead   Account   ‹ Collapse

0 filters applied   ⊼ Pin filters

Company   **Personal**

Company headcount 🚩	+		Connection 🚩	+
Current Company	+		Geography 🚩	+
Past Company	+		Industry 🚩	+
Company type	+		Years of experience 🚩	+
Company headquarters	+		Connections of	+
			Groups	+

Role

Current job title 🚩	+		First Name	+
Past job title 🚩	+		Last Name	+
Function	+		Profile language	+
Seniority level	+		TeamLink connections of	+
Years in current company	+		School	+
Years in current position	+

Workflow

| | | Lead lists 🚩 | + |

Spotlights

| Activities and shared experiences 🚩 | + |

People in CRM 🚩   +
To enable filter, upgrade contract

Posted Content

	Persona ⑦	+
Keyword in articles	+		Account lists	+
	People you interacted with	+
	Saved leads and accounts	+

When using the search function within Sales Navigator, it's essential to build your lists using relevant filters to narrow down the results to a manageable size. As you add each filter, the result list will decrease until you've created your ideal target list.

Once you have your list of your ideal clients, you can save that search. You also have the ability to "Save" (or follow) each relevant contact on that list. This action enables you to keep updated on their activities and interactions on LinkedIn, helping you stay relevant and informed in your engagement with them.

Spotlights (activities and shared experiences)

One filter that truly stands out for its value is Spotlights for both leads and accounts. Spotlights is a unique feature in Sales Navigator that helps you identify leads who are more likely to engage with you. By utilizing a variety of filters based on activities and shared experiences, Spotlights gives you a strategic edge in identifying and connecting with potential leads. Filters available within Spotlights include:

Changed jobs in last 90 days: This filter helps find people who may be interested in making an impression in their new role, making them more open to connecting if you can add value.

Mentioned in the news in last 30 days: This filter allows you to personalize your outreach based on recent news mentions.

Posted on LinkedIn in last 30 days: This filter prioritizes your outreach to leads who have recently posted on LinkedIn, providing insights on what's important to them. You can use this information to create a personal message or to engage with their content.

Following your company: This filter identifies leads who have followed or commented on your company's posts on LinkedIn, indicating potential interest.

Have shared experiences with you: This filter helps leverage common experiences to establish rapport in your outreach.

With TeamLink intro: This filter finds leads who are already connected to colleagues at your company, providing a potential path for warm introductions. (Only available with Advanced and Advanced Plus.)

With TeamLink intro through your executive: This filter identifies if an executive at your company has a relationship with a potential client that could provide a warm introduction. (Only available with Advanced and Advanced Plus.)

Past customer: This filter will help you uncover hidden allies by finding leads who worked at a company that has been your customer. This data is based on the opportunities in your CRM and is only available to Advanced Plus customers.

Past colleague: This filter identifies if a past colleague is now working at the company you're targeting, potentially providing introductions and insight on the best person(s) to reach out to.

Viewed your profile in last 90 days: This filter alerts you when a prospect has recently viewed your profile, providing an opportunity for you to send a personalized connection request.

Spotlights feature available for Accounts (companies)

In addition to the value Spotlights brings to individual lead search, Sales Navigator also offers additional features for Accounts (companies) with the Advanced and Advanced Plus subscription.

The "Buyer Intent Activities" filter includes actions taken by people within the targeted Account, such as LinkedIn ad engagement, InMail acceptance for a colleague, company LinkedIn page visits, or LinkedIn profile visits to colleagues and leadership. This feature demonstrates the power of Sales Navigator to not just focus on leads (individuals) but also on holistic account-based strategies.

Additional features in Sales Navigator

Beyond the advanced search function I've covered here, there are many additional features available within Sales Navigator that you can see in the chart I shared, showing the difference between Sales Navigator's Core, Advanced, and Advanced Plus plans. Consider investing in Sales Navigator if you're facing these challenges:

- Reaching the commercial search limit on free LinkedIn accounts.
- Wanting a customized newsfeed focused on targeted leads and accounts.
- Needing robust search filters and targeting options.
- Requiring in-depth profile visitor analytics.
- Looking for flexible lead list management and notes.
- Wanting to save and re-use successful searches.

Sales Navigator provides premium tools to find and engage prospects. Filters like company size and growth, years of experience, job changes, and spotlights help pinpoint precise prospects. You can save searches and get automatic updates when new prospects match your parameters daily, weekly, or monthly. With dozens of advanced filters, Sales Navigator enables superior search refinement and time savings.

From my experience, Sales Navigator is the clear choice for those active in social selling, providing robust targeting and sales specific tools.

Deciding on the Right LinkedIn Subscription

The free, Premium Business, and Sales Navigator plans provide varying levels of capabilities based on your needs. The free plan works well for basic networking and content sharing, while Premium Business unlocks more options for branding, lead generation, and networking. Sales Navigator provides robust tools tailored specifically for sales prospecting.

When selecting the right plan, assess your goals and anticipated usage. Those really active with social selling will get the most value from the targeting features in Sales Navigator. Premium Business gives marketers, business owners, and other professionals expanded reach and insights for branding and lead generation, though the sales-focused features are limited compared to Sales Navigator.

The free plan can be a good fit for more passive users focused on networking and building their personal brand through content sharing. For those seeking more business capabilities, Premium Business and Sales Navigator unlock greater functionality through expanded profile options, search filters, and analytics. However, the paid plans require evaluating expected utilization to warrant the investment.

Review the key features and typical usage across the plans to select the LinkedIn subscription that will provide the best ROI based on your professional needs.

When choosing the right LinkedIn subscription, first carefully evaluate your typical activities and goals on LinkedIn. Do you focus more on networking, content sharing, lead generation, or sales prospecting?

Next, compare your goals and ideal usage to the features and limitations of the free, Premium Business, and Sales Navigator plans outlined in this chapter. If unsure, take advantage of the free trials to experience the premium features firsthand. During the trial, track your usage to determine the potential ROI of investing in a paid subscription.

With this thorough evaluation process, you can determine the optimal LinkedIn plan to maximize the value of your LinkedIn presence and investment. The right subscription can provide immense returns by connecting you with the right people, resources, and opportunities for your business and career growth.

Why Sales Navigator Deserves Special Attention

As you've learned, Sales Navigator offers features beyond the free and Premium Business versions, specifically aimed at sales professionals. If your role is primarily in sales or business development, and especially if you're focusing on mid- to large-sized companies, you might feel that this chapter just scratches the surface. That's intentional.

If you're a sales professional who sells to mid- to large-sized companies and you want to unlock the full potential of Sales Navigator, consider picking up my specialized book, *Navigating LinkedIn for Sales*. This book dives deep into the intricacies of complex selling, account-based marketing, and maximizing Sales Navigator for greater success.

LinkedIn offers various subscription plans to meet different needs. Choosing the right one can dramatically enhance your social selling strategy. Follow these steps to select the best fit:

Step 1: Audit Your Usage: Track your current LinkedIn activities and identify your primary objectives. Are you focused on networking, content sharing, lead generation, or sales prospecting? Be clear on how you currently use LinkedIn.

Step 2: Compare the Plans: Make a side-by-side comparison of the key features and limitations of the free, Premium Business, and Sales Navigator plans. Consider which aligns best with your goals and needs.

Step 3: Start a Free Trial: If you haven't decided on a plan yet, take advantage of LinkedIn's free trials of Premium Business or Sales Navigator. Evaluate the expanded features and track your usage to determine the potential ROI.

Bonus Action Step: If you're in sales or business development and already using Sales Navigator, upgrade your strategy by getting a copy of *Navigating LinkedIn for Sales*. You'll find this book to be a more in-depth guide to conquering complex sales scenarios and mastering Sales Navigator.

Selecting the optimal LinkedIn subscription is crucial for social selling success. The following chapters will cover how to maximize your chosen plan through effective content, conversations, and prospecting.

PART TWO

STRATEGIES

CHAPTER FIVE

Master LinkedIn Etiquette and Best Practices

When it comes to LinkedIn, there are specific rules and guidelines. Understanding and playing by these rules is crucial if you want to win at social selling. In this chapter, I'll break down these rules, guidelines, and best practices, and give you straightforward tips for using LinkedIn to find leads and build a solid reputation and personal brand.

Turning a blind eye to these basic rules can lead to trouble, like restrictions on your account or even getting banned from the platform altogether. That's why I want to help you navigate through both the official and unspoken dos and don'ts of LinkedIn and social selling. I'll also point out the common mistakes you need to avoid, including the types of posts that could harm your professional image.

LinkedIn Etiquette and Best Practices

This section dives into the heart of LinkedIn etiquette, providing you with essential insights into the best practices to make the most of this professional platform, while maintaining credibility and building genuine connections.

Personalize

Personalization is indispensable when approaching social selling on LinkedIn. Each connection request you send should be tailored to the individual. It's crucial to take the time to research your prospects and compose personalized connection requests. Such attention to detail can and does make a significant difference, often determining whether someone clicks "Accept" or "Ignore" in response to your request.

Sending an impersonal invite might lead the recipient to select "I don't know this person," risking account restrictions if reported frequently. Such a restriction could severely impact your ability to connect with prospects and expand your network.

In the world of LinkedIn and social selling, personalization is not optional. Since most people neglect to personalize, adhering to this one tip will drastically enhance your success on LinkedIn, making your invite stand out. I'll cover more on how to do this well in an upcoming chapter.

Respond to messages promptly

On LinkedIn, your response time to messages can influence your relationships with potential clients and valuable connections. Make it a priority to reply promptly, to show that you value their time and are interested in engaging with them.

In addition, always make sure to read and fully understand the message before responding. Take the time to craft a thoughtful and personalized response that directly addresses the content of the message. This will demonstrate your professionalism and help build trust with your potential clients.

Utilize the "Who's Viewed Your Profile" feature

Utilizing the "Who's Viewed Your Profile" feature is a powerful tool in social selling. By checking this section regularly, you can identify potential leads who have already shown an interest in your profile.

In addition to identifying the viewers of your profile, you can also gain valuable insights into their companies, industries, and locations. With a paid LinkedIn membership like Premium Business or Sales Navigator, you can see everyone who has viewed your profile. A free basic account only allows you to see the last five viewers.

Regularly reviewing this information can help you understand who your profile and LinkedIn content are attracting. If you are not receiving many profile views, following the best practices outlined in this book will increase your visibility and attract more viewers to your profile.

When reaching out to someone who has viewed your profile, make sure to personalize your connection request and avoid mentioning that you saw they viewed your profile. This approach will help you establish a genuine connection and increase the likelihood of a positive response.

Avoid sending irrelevant (spam) messages

Avoid sending irrelevant messages to your connections on LinkedIn, as it can harm your relationship with prospects. This can be defined as anything the receiver doesn't derive value from, which many consider a form of spam. Ensure every message you send is entirely relevant; otherwise, recipients will ignore you, or worse, flag you as a spammer.

It's important to keep in mind that everything you send to your connections should be positioned for their benefit, not yours. Avoid sales-related and irrelevant messages, as this will damage your reputation and credibility, and you will not get a second chance.

Ensure your profile passes their "what's in it for me?" test

If you want your profile to resonate with your ideal clients, it must answer their primary question: "What's in it for me?" The reality is, people aren't too concerned with you, your company, or your products/services. What they care about is their problems and how you can help them.

When prospects check out your profile, they're looking for signs that you're the solution to their problems. Therefore, your profile should be like a welcome mat that assures them they're in the right place. Make it crystal clear that you understand their specific challenges and that you're the right person to help them overcome those.

Keep your Name field clean

Using anything other than your real name—like email addresses, phone numbers, or symbols—is not just against LinkedIn's rules, but can prevent people from easily finding you. And it certainly won't enhance your professional image. There are exceptions, though. Suffixes, former names, maiden names, or nicknames are fine if people who know you can still recognize you.

Write like you are chatting face-to-face

One of the best tips I can give you is to always write as you would speak if you were in front of a potential client.

When you are sending any kind of message to a LinkedIn connection, read it out loud. Would you speak like that if you were standing in front of them? If not, revise your message.

By communicating in a natural, genuine manner, you're more likely to connect with potential clients. Keep the jargon to a minimum and avoid excessively formal language. Your aim should be to make your language straightforward and relatable.

Leverage voice notes

Adding a personal touch to your LinkedIn communication can be as simple as using voice notes. Unlike written text, voice notes let you share your message in a more authentic, personalized way, helping build trust and rapport with your prospects.

Voice notes let your communication skills shine and help you stand out. Plus, they're quicker than typing, so they can be especially handy when you're scheduling a call or following up on a lead.

But remember, there's a right way to use voice messages. Always introduce yourself, explain why you're reaching out, and make sure your message is clear and concise. Keep it brief; a lengthy message might be too time-consuming for your prospect to listen to. One word of caution: voice notes shouldn't be used until you've had at least one interaction with a prospect. If you use them too soon, they will likely be ignored.

Nurture your relationships on LinkedIn

Engage with your LinkedIn connections regularly to nurture your relationships. LinkedIn will notify you of alerts, such as when a connection starts a new job or is mentioned in the news. This provides a natural way of striking up a conversation.

Stay tuned to your newsfeed for additional opportunities to engage with your network. If you see them post something, leave a thoughtful comment when relevant. Anytime you come across a resource, article, or news piece that would be of interest to someone you know, share it with them directly in a private message.

When people engage with your content, whether by commenting or sharing, always respond. Thank them for their engagement and participation in the conversation. Take a page out of Bob Burg's book and use LinkedIn the "go-giver way:" Create value, make an impact, expand your network, be genuine, and stay open. Providing consistent value to your connections builds long-lasting relationships that will benefit both you and your business in the long run.

Never add your LinkedIn connections to your email list without their permission

Never add your LinkedIn connections to your email list, even if you've received their email address through LinkedIn messaging. Adding someone to your marketing email list without their permission is illegal in some countries, as well as a violation of LinkedIn's terms of service. It can damage the credibility and reputation of both you and your company. It can also result in them reporting your email as spam, which can harm your deliverability rates and result in penalties.

Embrace positivity and professionalism

It's essential to maintain a positive and professional tone on LinkedIn. Avoid criticizing anyone publicly or expressing negative opinions about your competitors. Remember, LinkedIn is a professional networking platform, not a space for personal disputes, like is often seen on some other social media sites. Disrespectful behavior on LinkedIn is a reputation killer. While sharing personal content is allowed, keep it to a minimum and always bear in mind who your audience is on LinkedIn.

LINKEDIN PRO TIP

Consider deactivating the "Viewers of this profile also viewed" option, which you'll find in the "Settings & Privacy" section. By default, LinkedIn often displays profiles of your competitors alongside yours. Turning off this setting is a smart move to prevent inadvertently directing people to check out your competitors' profiles.

Essential Skills You Need to Succeed with Social Selling

To excel at social selling, you need more than just best practices and LinkedIn etiquette. Some critical skills can significantly amplify your success, many of which are basic life lessons we learned in childhood. Let's explore seven essential skills to utilize in your social selling journey.

Politeness always pays: Recognize the importance of basic manners and etiquette in your social selling activities. Simple gestures, like saying "please" and "thank you" or expressing appreciation when someone engages with your posts, can lay the foundation for strong, positive relationships.

Learn from mistakes: Don't let the fear of mistakes hold you back from experimenting with LinkedIn and taking some risks. Everyone stumbles at some point. The key is to acknowledge it, learn from these moments, and use them as stepping stones to growth.

Encourage collaboration: Collaboration is a powerful instrument for building a strong network. LinkedIn provides an excellent platform to connect with potential partners offering complementary products or services. Always be on the lookout for opportunities to create win-win situations.

Be generous: Showing generosity can significantly boost your social selling results. Whether it's sharing insightful content from your network or helping a connection overcome a problem, giving without expecting anything in return can breed goodwill and solidify relationships.

Question, listen, then engage: Spark conversations by asking thoughtful questions and showing genuine interest in your connections' responses. Active involvement leads to meaningful discussions, setting the stage for strong relationships and potential business opportunities.

Be patient and persistent: Remember, social selling is more of a marathon than a sprint. Building trust, cultivating relationships, and securing deals all take time. If you don't see immediate results, don't lose heart or give up. Maintain consistency, follow up regularly, and continuously nurture your connections.

Adapt and innovate: Social selling isn't a "one-size-fits-all" game. You need to stay flexible, monitor what's working (and what's not), and adapt your strategies as needed. Being open to new ideas and learning from your experiences will ensure you stay ahead in the ever-evolving world of social selling.

Navigating Common Pitfalls in Social Selling

Though social selling is an effective and efficient method of building business relationships and driving sales, some obstacles can limit its effectiveness. Understanding these potential challenges can help you avoid them and get the most out of your social selling efforts. Here are some common pitfalls to watch out for:

Over-selling: While it might be tempting to push for immediate sales, remember that social selling is about building relationships. Coming off too strong with aggressive selling can deter potential clients. Focus instead on understanding and fulfilling your connections' needs, positioning yourself as a helpful resource rather than trying to push a sale.

Inconsistency: Consistency is a key factor in social selling. If you're sporadically posting and engaging, it can make you appear unreliable and unengaged. Try to maintain a regular presence by posting consistently and engaging with your connections.

Ignoring personal branding: Your personal brand serves as your unique value proposition. Failure to define and communicate this can lead to missed connections and opportunities. Ensure your LinkedIn profile and other platforms clearly showcase your skills, values, and credibility.

One-way communication: Remember, social selling is about engaging in conversations, not just broadcasting your message. Make sure to listen and respond to comments, messages, and inquiries from your network.

Resistance to change: The digital landscape is constantly evolving. If you don't adapt and update your strategies based on new trends, tools, and platforms, you could fall behind. Stay open to learning and be ready to modify your approach as needed.

Lack of goals: Without specific goals, your social selling efforts can be hard to focus on and plan. It's important to set goals that are SMART (Specific, Measurable, Achievable, Relevant, Time-bound) to guide your strategy and measure your progress.

Not doing your homework: Engaging with prospects without doing your research can result in generic and impersonal interactions. Try to understand your prospects' needs and interests so you can tailor your content and interactions to be as relevant and impactful as possible.

Ignoring analytics: LinkedIn provides valuable insights into who is interacting with your content and how. Disregarding these insights means missing out on opportunities to refine your strategy based on what's working and what isn't.

Focusing solely on online relationships: While building online relationships is an important step in the social selling process, the goal is to move those conversations offline. Sales conversations should only happen once you've booked an appointment (phone, video call, face-to-face), as only then do you have a chance to learn enough information to convert a prospect into a client.

LinkedIn Features You Might Be Neglecting

LinkedIn is more than just a platform for posting updates and sending and accepting connection requests. To fully leverage the platform's potential, it's essential to be aware of and effectively use its many features. Here are some key functionalities you might be underutilizing.

Publishing LinkedIn Newsletters: Starting your own newsletter series on LinkedIn can be a valuable touchpoint with your audience. It allows you to share in-depth insights on topics you're an expert in, and regularly engage with your connections. It's a fantastic way to offer additional value and stimulate ongoing engagement.

Creating long-form content: LinkedIn supports the creation and publication of long-form content. By investing time in crafting comprehensive articles, you can showcase your industry knowledge and position yourself as an authority on your topic.

Hosting LinkedIn Live or Audio Events: LinkedIn Live and Audio Events allow you to host real-time events like Q&As or interviews with experts. This encourages high engagement levels and offers the chance to connect personally with your audience.

Engaging with others' content: This isn't just about posts made by your target market, but also their comments on others' posts. Participating in these discussions can significantly enhance your visibility and credibility within your network.

Posting videos: Video content is highly engaging and can significantly increase visibility and engagement on your profile. You can create and share educational content, explainer videos, product demonstrations, customer testimonials, or even short clips that provide valuable insights to your network.

Taking advantage of LinkedIn Learning: Available with any paid subscription, LinkedIn Learning offers a wealth of educational courses across a wide range of subjects. By regularly investing in your learning and development, you can acquire new skills that add value to your profile and offer more to your network.

Using LinkedIn Polls: LinkedIn Polls is a feature that allows you to gauge the opinion of your network on a certain topic. It's a great way to engage your connections, generate discussions, and gain valuable insights about your industry or audience. However, be careful not to overuse this feature, because anything that is used too much will stop working eventually.

Remember, the key to success on LinkedIn is consistent and meaningful engagement. By using many of the tools and features available, you can maximize your reach and influence on the platform.

Mastering Content Sharing on LinkedIn: Strategic Practices and What to Avoid

Building a credible personal brand and establishing yourself as an authority on LinkedIn requires consistent sharing of high-quality content. However, the art of content sharing is more nuanced than it seems at first. Let's cover some best practices and pitfalls to avoid helping you maximize reach and engagement with your network.

Sharing Content Strategically

Quality, consistency, and strategic timing are key when sharing content on LinkedIn. Ensure your posts are well-written, informative, and resonate with your target audience. A consistent posting schedule helps build momentum and credibility.

Using LinkedIn features like @mentions, #hashtags, and even emojis can enhance engagement. @mentions enable you to tag specific individuals or companies, while #hashtags aid in content discoverability. Emojis can add a dash of personality to your posts, provided they're not overused. Lastly, incorporating calls to action can boost engagement and visibility.

Experiment with a variety of content topics, voices, and formats to keep your audience intrigued. From personal to business topics, inspirational to aspirational voices, and text updates to visual narratives, a diverse content strategy can go a long way.

Performance Analysis

Monitoring key performance metrics like engagement rates and leads generated is vital to assess the efficacy of your content strategy. LinkedIn's analytics dashboard offers insights into post performance, including impressions, reactions, comments, and reposts. Plus, you'll find the top demographics of your viewers, including company size, job titles, locations, companies, and industries. Use this data to refine your content strategy and optimize your posts for maximum impact.

What to Steer Clear From

While LinkedIn provides a platform for a variety of content, maintaining a professional demeanor is crucial. Completely avoid the following types of posts:

- **Controversial and shaming posts**: Polarizing content, posts, or comments shaming others will hinder relationship building and harm your personal brand. They often lead to a divisive mentality.
- **Political or religious posts**: These can elicit strong positions, potentially causing offense and friction with prospects if your beliefs diverge from theirs.

- **Inappropriate personal posts**: Personal posts can add authenticity to your LinkedIn profile, allowing you to connect on a more human level with your network. However, it's crucial to maintain a professional tone. Be cautious with posts that could be interpreted as unprofessional, as they may not be well-received in a business-oriented environment like LinkedIn.

Common Mistakes to Avoid

Certain practices can inadvertently harm your personal brand. Posting too frequently can appear spammy, while scarce posts may indicate inactivity.

Being overly promotional is another common misstep. While product or service promotion is acceptable, it's essential to add value for your audience in the process.

LinkedIn Creator Mode

LinkedIn Creator Mode is a feature that can help you increase your visibility and reach on the platform. By enabling Creator Mode, your profile will be better optimized for content creation and promotion, showcasing your latest and most relevant content at the top of your profile. But how can you specifically benefit from this feature?

Leveraging Creator Mode can empower you to display your expertise, share industry-specific insights, expand your audience, and utilize analytics. Enabling Creator Mode also unlocks additional features like publishing a LinkedIn Newsletter and using LinkedIn Live or Audio Events. Even if you're not interested in these features, enabling Creator Mode could still be beneficial for featuring select content prominently on your profile. However, it's not a one-size-fits-all solution and should only be activated if you're comfortable with regularly creating and sharing content. If you're game for it, here are some tips to maximize LinkedIn Creator Mode:

- **Optimize your profile:** Before enabling Creator Mode, make sure your LinkedIn profile is updated and professional. This includes having a professional headshot, a clear and concise headline, a well-crafted About section that highlights your expertise, and a completed Experience section.

- **Feature valuable content:** With Creator Mode, your content is prominently featured on your profile, so it's important to make sure you're sharing content that resonates with your target audience. This includes sharing industry-specific news, trends, and insights, as well as your own unique perspectives and experiences.

- **Choose your five topics, displayed as #hashtags:** Display five hashtags on your profile that allow viewers to know what topics you consistently discuss.

- **Include a link to where you want people to go**: Display a link that sends people to your company website, LinkedIn newsletter, landing page, or anywhere else you want to highlight.

- **Review and monitor your analytics:** Creator Mode offers deeper insights, such as post impressions, profile views, followers, and search appearances. Regular monitoring of these analytics can guide your content strategy.

By leveraging these tips, you can significantly enhance your visibility on LinkedIn, showcase your expertise effectively, and attract more leads. If you feel ready and confident, enable Creator Mode and start creating, curating, and promoting your value-rich content.

Measure What Matters

It is important to know what you are trying to achieve on LinkedIn, and understanding social selling often requires a different perspective and set of indicators. The number of likes or connections you amass is less important than the relationships you nurture and the value you contribute. The following metrics can provide a more holistic view of your social selling effectiveness.

Engagement: How many comments, likes, and shares do your posts generate? Are people interested in the content you're sharing, and are they willing to engage in meaningful conversations with you? Look for trends in your posts that resonate with your audience, and aim to create more posts like that.

Content quality: Is your content useful, interesting, and relevant to your audience? This metric may be harder to quantify, but you can gauge it through the feedback and engagement your content receives.

Connection quality: Are you connected to the right people? Not just potential clients, but also industry leaders, influencers, and others who can contribute to your learning and development as a professional.

Inbound messages: Are people reaching out to you based on your activity and presence on LinkedIn? This is a strong indicator of your influence on the platform.

Response rate: Are prospects responding to the messages you're sending? Sales is a numbers game, but evaluating your response rates will tell you a lot about the quality of your messages and how they're being received.

Conversion rate: How many of your LinkedIn connections have you been able to move to offline conversations? Tracking this conversion rate can help you identify the success of your social selling efforts.

By focusing on these metrics, you're ensuring that your LinkedIn presence goes beyond just "being active" to building meaningful relationships and positioning yourself as an authority in your field.

As you redefine your social selling success on LinkedIn, remember that patience is key. The process of building relationships and establishing authority takes time. Stay consistent in your efforts, continue to learn and adapt, and watch your network grow and your sales thrive.

ACTION PLAN

By this point, you should be grasping the potential of LinkedIn as an invaluable resource for social selling. To get the most out of this platform, follow these action steps:

Step 1: Initiate Genuine Conversations: Create meaningful interactions on LinkedIn by initiating genuine conversations, leaving insightful comments, and sharing knowledge that brings value to your network. Start by commenting on a few posts shared by your connections.

Step 2: Utilize LinkedIn Features: LinkedIn offers a range of features across its free, Premium, and Sales Navigator versions. Ensure you are using functions that align with your social selling strategy. Dedicate time to understanding how these features can empower your sales efforts, and utilize them to their maximum potential.

Step 3: Define Your LinkedIn Goals: Become clear on what you will measure on LinkedIn. Set the goals you wish to achieve and the metrics you will use to measure them.

This book will cover more about how to initiate conversations, share content effectively, and utilize a variety of LinkedIn features, so please keep an eye out for those in future chapters.

CHAPTER SIX

Find Leads and Prospects on LinkedIn

In Chapter 3, I walked you through how to create a client-centric LinkedIn profile, which reads as a resource for your prospects rather than a resume. Having this client-centric profile in place is essential before you begin utilizing LinkedIn to find, connect, and build a relationship with your prospects.

Once you are ready to begin locating your ideal clients, you can take advantage of LinkedIn's Advanced Search function. The amount and types of filters available to you will depend upon which LinkedIn subscription you have. Sales Navigator offers the most robust set of filters and saving capabilities to do the kinds of targeted searches that allow you to zero in on the right leads and decision-makers. You can still do very targeted searches with a free or Premium Business account, but you'll have fewer search filters available to you.

If you use everything you learn in this book, the chances are high that you'll exceed LinkedIn's commercial use limits, which impacts the number of searches you can perform each month. These limits are triggered when your usage exceeds normal search activity, such as hiring or prospecting. You'll get a warning as you get closer to the limit. If you exceed it, your free monthly usage won't reset until the first day of the next calendar month.

As we explore the benefits and functions of LinkedIn, I'll start by explaining how to leverage LinkedIn's free capabilities, and then I'll expand the discussion to describe the additional capabilities you can access through Sales Navigator.

Using LinkedIn's Advanced Search

The **Search** bar, located in the top-left corner of every page, allows you to start your search for people, companies, jobs, posts, and more. For our purposes here, we'll be focusing on searching for **People** and **Companies**.

After you've started your search, you'll see several tabs you can use to refine your results. The most useful filters for sales include:

People: Select from your 1st, 2nd, and/or 3rd-degree connections when searching. Your 1st-degree connections are people you are directly connected to. It is typically your 2nd-degree connections (the connections of your connections) that you'll want to target, as your 3rd-degree connections are too far removed, and people will often not accept a connection request unless you share some mutual connections with them.

Once you've selected a people search, you can further narrow it down to specific locations. This is very valuable if you are focusing on getting business from a specific geographical area.

Companies: If you are focused on landing specific companies as clients, you can filter specifically for the companies you are interested in.

Once you click on an individual company's page, there will be lots of valuable information available by clicking on any of the tabs such as Posts, Jobs, People, Insights, etc.

From the company page, if you select "People" at a quick glance, you'll be able to see where the employees live, where and what they studied, what they do, what they are skilled at, and how you are connected. In this same section, you'll find a search bar where you can search for employees by title, keyword, or school.

Keyword filters

To further refine your search, use specific keywords to narrow down your results. LinkedIn currently allows you to filter using keywords in the first or last name, job title, company, and school fields.

Boolean search

In addition to search filters, you can also use Boolean search operators as part of your search, a type of shorthand using symbols that tells a search engine to do highly specific things. Let's say you want to find product managers under the title filter, and you use that as a keyword in your search. Your search results would pull up people who have the words "product" and/or "manager" in their profile, not necessarily together. By adding quotation marks around "product manager" when typing in the keyword, you are telling the search engine to show you only results containing those two words specifically together.

Here is a summary of the most common Boolean operators. As a bonus, these operators work in most search engines on the Internet, not just LinkedIn's.

QUOTATION MARKS

If you would like to search for an exact phrase, you can enclose the phrase in quotation marks. You can use these in addition to other modifiers.

Example: `"mechanical engineer"`

AND

If you would like to search for profiles that include two terms, you can separate those terms with the uppercase word AND. However, you don't have to use AND—if you enter two terms, the search program will assume that there is an AND between them.

Example: "VP Sales" AND "Director Sales"

OR

If you would like to broaden your search to find profiles that include one or more terms, you can separate those terms with the uppercase word OR.

Example: "account executive" OR "account exec" OR "account manager" OR "sales executive" OR "sales manager"

PARENTHESES

If you would like to do a complex search, you can combine terms and modifiers. For example, this phrase will find both VPs of Sales and Directors of Sales:

(VP OR Director) AND Sales

NOT

If you would like to do a search but exclude a particular term, type that term with an uppercase NOT immediately before it. Your search results will exclude any profile containing that term. So, for example, if you were looking for a CEO of a larger company, not a small business owner, founder, or consultant, you could use the phrase:

CEO NOT Owner NOT Founder NOT Consultant

To show you the true power of Boolean operators when combined, imagine that you want to search for directors, but only at Microsoft or IBM, but not if they are vice presidents. A search for that would say:

```
Director (Microsoft OR IBM) NOT "Vice
President"
```

Using a Boolean search can help you narrow down your search and provide more targeted results, although it doesn't guarantee that every person who comes up will be perfectly targeted. To further refine your search, you can continue to narrow down by location, company, and other filters until you find precisely what you want.

It's important to note that when looking for new opportunities, you should remove 1st-degree connections from your search parameters, as they are already part of your network. Instead, focus on finding 2nd-degree connections who can see that you have connections in common.

Search by job opportunities

Searching by "Jobs" from a company page can be an effective way to conduct research and gain insights into the company's growth, financial stability, and current needs or challenges. By using different keywords, you can also learn about the projects or skills the company is currently hiring for, which can provide valuable information on their growth trajectory and current priorities.

Network with alumni

If you've graduated from a university or college, you have a valuable network of people you can easily connect with, as you share something in common. LinkedIn offers an easy way to gather valuable intel on the alumni from your university or college, including similar information available about the people in a company, such as:

- Where they work
- Where they live
- What they do
- What they are skilled at
- What they studied
- How you are connected

To check your university or college alumni page, go to www.linkedin.com/alumni, which will take you to the most recent educational institution you attended. Alternatively, you can search for your educational institution on LinkedIn and find the Alumni page.

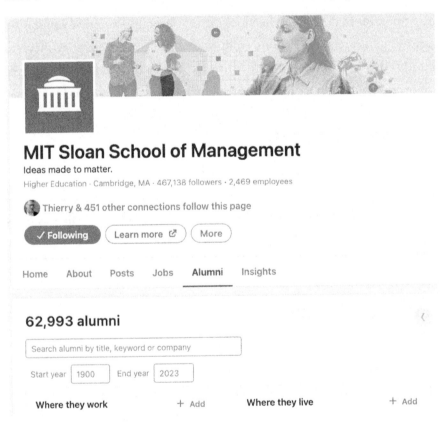

MIT Sloan School of Management
Ideas made to matter.
Higher Education · Cambridge, MA · 467,138 followers · 2,469 employees

Thierry & 451 other connections follow this page

(✓ Following) (Learn more ⬀) (More)

Home   About   Posts   Jobs   **Alumni**   Insights

62,993 alumni

Search alumni by title, keyword or company

Start year [1900]   End year [2023]

Where they work   + Add   **Where they live**   + Add

Using the search box on the alumni page, you can search by name, title, company, or keyword to find individuals from specific companies you may want to connect with. Although you share an educational institution, this does not guarantee that the person will be receptive. However, fellow alumni are more likely to reply to a connection request due to your shared experience.

In your personalized connection request message, mention the alumni connection at the beginning of the message, be polite and professional, and show that you've done your research on them. This demonstrates that you are not sending out a generic message. The goal is to establish a connection, and once that is done, you can further the conversation through a follow-up message.

Prospect Profile Research

While many LinkedIn members are active or at least semi-active on the platform, there are also many users who rarely or never use the platform after creating their personal profile. Therefore, it's important to do a quick assessment of their personal profile to see if they regularly use the platform before trying to engage with them there. This can save you time and energy.

In addition to determining their activity on LinkedIn, a quick profile scan can provide you with other valuable information you can use when you reach out to engage or connect with that person. When you find a person who matches the criteria you've set, take a closer look at their profile and gather information such as:

- What if any content or posts have they recently shared or commented on?
- What does their About section reveal about them?
- What is their current role and responsibilities?
- What are their publicized interests outside of work?
- If they have a personal website/blog, what are they posting?

Compiling this information will help inform how you approach your outreach. Another helpful indicator when trying to determine if someone is active on LinkedIn is to look for a Premium subscription (represented by a gold badge with the word "IN"). These people are often more receptive to receiving messages and new connection requests.

Determining someone's network size

Determining the size of a someone's network on LinkedIn can also help gauge their activity level on the platform. If a LinkedIn member has less than 500 connections, the exact number of their connections is shown. However, if they have more than 500 connections, LinkedIn will display "500+" instead of the exact number.

To estimate the number of connections of those with more than 500, you can look at the number of followers they have under the Activity section on their profile. With some people this number is often similar to their number of connections, since 1st-degree connections are automatically followers. However, keep in mind that well-known influencers, high-level executives, or those who post engaging content may have significantly more followers than connections.

It's important to note that LinkedIn has a cap of 30,000 connections for all members. If someone has more than 30,000 followers, the excess count consists of followers, not actual connections. Overall, those with thousands of connections or followers tend to be more active on the platform than those with less than 500, and thus more likely to be receptive to a connection request.

Following vs. Connecting

While you ultimately want to connect with an individual, there may be situations where it will be more effective to initially follow them and not immediately send them a personalized connection request.

There will be times when you need to establish your authority or at the very least establish some familiarity before you reach out with a connection request, especially with high-level decision makers or industry influencers. In these cases, you might want to start by following that person. Following someone on LinkedIn allows you to see their posts and what they are engaging with on your newsfeed, without being connected to them.

By following these people, you can pay attention to what is currently important to them, the challenges they may be facing, and the language they're using to speak about those things. They're also notified that you're following them. To begin making yourself more familiar with them and slowly establish some credibility, you can begin to engage, when appropriate, with their posts and comments. This can be a great way to start a conversation with them. But your engagement must make sense and must NEVER be sales-related. It's important to note that the people you follow won't see your posts, which makes it important for you to work toward sending them a connection request and becoming part of their 1st-degree network.

To follow a LinkedIn member who does not have the "Follow" button enabled, go to the person's profile and click on the "More" option (or "..." on LinkedIn Mobile) and select "Follow."

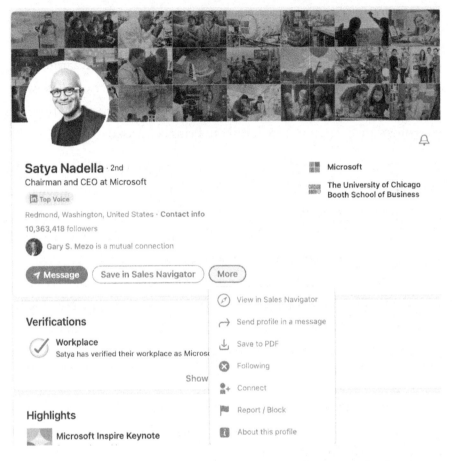

Even if you choose to send a connection request right away, take the time to follow all the accounts (company pages) and individuals (personal profiles) you've defined as viable prospects. This will allow you to gain insights into them and what they are sharing on LinkedIn.

Supercharge Your Prospecting with Sales Navigator

If you want to streamline your lead generation and get more valuable insights on prospects, you may instead choose to use Sales Navigator. Before I discuss this in detail, though, for disclosure's sake please note that I have no vested interest in advocating for Sales Navigator, and don't use affiliate links in my writing. However, for those serious about lead generation, I have found it to be a tremendous resource. Investing in this platform translates into saving precious time, unlocking critical insights, and achieving significantly better outreach results.

While Sales Navigator offers many benefits and can be a valuable tool for those focused on lead generation, it's important to note that it may not be the right choice for everyone. Carefully evaluate whether the investment in Sales Navigator aligns with your specific goals and strategies, and most importantly how you plan to use LinkedIn specifically. Perhaps your goal is simply to build a stronger personal brand and position yourself as an authority through content; for that, Sales Navigator is not necessary.

That said, if lead generation is a priority and you are not fully utilizing Sales Navigator (or not using it at all), you may be leaving valuable opportunities on the table and expending unnecessary effort. Sales Navigator is equipped with exhaustive search capabilities and personalized newsfeeds.

Additional Sales Navigator Capabilities

In addition to the robust Advanced Search Sales Navigator provides for both people and companies (which I covered in detail in Chapter 4), including the incredibly valuable Spotlights filter, there are several other features that could be of interest to you.

Personas

Personas, as a feature in Sales Navigator, are valuable for streamlining your searches and creating even more effective outreaches. Using the personas filter, you can tailor your Sales Navigator experience around attributes of your target individuals, such as job title and function, and hone in your efforts on your ideal clients.

With a few clicks, you can define your target persona. This persona is then highlighted on the homepage, in search, in Relationship Explorer, and on account pages. The feature also offers demographic insights indicating whether the persona is growing or shrinking at a particular account.

Growth Insights Available for Accounts

If you are targeting larger companies, Sales Navigator provides valuable insights to help you understand a company's growth, including:

- Employee count
- Distribution & headcount
- New hires
- Job openings
- Personas

Each insight casts a light on the company's current standing, enabling you to fine-tune your outreach strategy. For instance, an increase in employee count might indicate that a company is open to fresh ideas and products, offering a prime opportunity for you to introduce your solutions. A high number of job openings might signal imminent expansion, suggesting that this could be a high-value prospect to focus on. Getting familiar with the company's personas can aid you in pinpointing decision makers and influencers, allowing you to customize your outreach to resonate with them.

Each insight you gain is a piece of the puzzle, painting a comprehensive picture of your prospect's growth and potential needs, allowing you to approach them strategically.

Saved Searches

Saved searches are a key feature of Sales Navigator that can significantly improve your efficiency. By saving your search criteria, you can quickly open your saved search without having to manually re-enter all the search filters each time. This capability saves you substantial time and effort in finding and connecting with leads.

Sales Navigator also offers alerts to keep you informed about new leads that match your search criteria. This feature ensures that you never miss an opportunity and can respond promptly to emerging leads.

To maximize your lead generation efforts on Sales Navigator, create a specific search that represents your hottest group of leads, then use the Spotlights filter to fine-tune your selection. For example, you can use the Spotlights filter to only include people who have posted on LinkedIn in the past 30 days. By doing this, LinkedIn will email you every day with a list of your hottest leads who have just posted something on LinkedIn, providing you with an engagement opportunity to initiate communication.

The Pro Tip here? Don't just use the tool, but leverage its features to ensure it works in your favor, facilitating prompt and effective engagement with prospects.

Saving Leads and Accounts

After running a search that produces promising results, you can sift through the search findings and start saving any relevant leads or accounts. This process enables you to swiftly scan through the results the search provides, saving potential leads into a temporary list for detailed evaluation at a later stage. You can then revisit and resave the most promising ones, storing them in a more definitive list.

To align with your workflow, you can customize the names of each of your lists. You might designate these lists with titles that describe the nature of the leads or accounts they contain, such as "Individuals who have changed jobs in the past 90 days," "Members who have posted on LinkedIn in the past 30 days," or "Companies experiencing senior leadership changes in the past 3 months."

To save a lead in Sales Navigator, execute your preferred search. When you spot a potential lead, click the "Save" button located to the right of their profile box. You can then select an existing list or create a new one by clicking the "+ Create lead list" option and assigning a name to your new list.

Creating Effective Searches

To craft an effective ideal client search, it's crucial to delve deeper than basic search filters like title, function, and geographical location. Here's how you can leverage your past and current relationships to discover new opportunities.

Reconnect with Previous Customers

Former satisfied customers are often open to doing business again, even at a different company, due to their familiarity with your products or services. In Sales Navigator's search feature, apply the "Past company" filter within the "Company" filter. This strategy allows you to track down employees associated with your past or present customers and uncover their current employers. This simple yet effective approach could unveil potential future business opportunities.

Company

Company headcount 📌	+
Current company ⊙	+
Past company ⊙	+
Company type	+
Company headquarters location	+

Gain Insights from Former Employees

An effective strategy to gather insights about a prospect's company is by leveraging the "Current company" and "Past company" filters. This allows you to locate individuals who once worked for the company you're targeting but are currently employed at your own company. Reaching out to these colleagues can provide valuable information and unique business insights about whom to engage at the targeted company, and may even facilitate introductions to the right contacts.

The more strategic and refined your searches are, the higher your chances are of identifying and engaging with your ideal clients.

Company

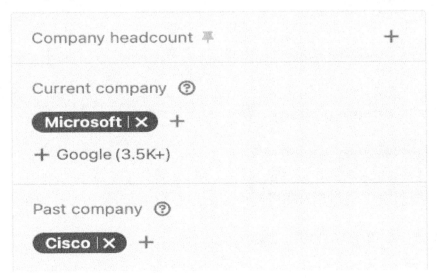

Prospect Personal Profile

Leveraging Sales Navigator to its fullest potential involves understanding the depth of insight provided by an individual's personal profile. This is more than just understanding their role, current employer, or previous job titles—it's about using this rich profile data to build relationships and find common ground.

The top section of a profile in Sales Navigator offers a comprehensive snapshot of an individual. It provides you with their current and past employment, recent activity, shared connections, and even the last time you interacted with them on Sales Navigator.

The "Notes" feature is your personal space to jot down details or reminders about the lead, while the "Save" function lets you segment leads into custom lists based on certain criteria.

By effectively utilizing these features, you can proficiently track, manage, and categorize your leads and accounts, thereby driving increased sales opportunities.

Custom Lists

Custom lists are a powerful tool for staying organized and optimizing your workflow. They can be used to filter contacts based on their stage in your outreach process. Here are several ways to leverage custom lists:

- **Filter by how you initially engaged the person:** This could include leads from events, webinars, or social media campaigns.
- **Filter by geographical location, the role they play in the decision-making process, and their interest in your product or service:** This helps you to better target and personalize your outreach to these leads based on their location, job title, and interest in your product or service.
- **Prioritize based on importance:** This helps you to prioritize your outreach and focus on the people or companies that are most important to your business.
- **Update the custom list when your relationship with an account or lead changes:** As your relationship with an account or lead changes, you can update the custom list to reflect this change.
- **Filter based on what stage they are in your outreach:** You can use custom lists to filter your contacts based on where they are in your outreach, such as initial outreach, follow-up, or nurturing. This helps you to stay organized and ensure that you are providing each lead with the appropriate level of attention. I'll share more on this in Chapters 7 and 10.

CUSTOM LISTS PRO TIP

To easily prioritize and access your most frequently used custom list, simply add a "#" before the list's name. This moves it to the top of your lists when sorted alphabetically. This trick is particularly helpful when you have many lists and need to find the ones you use the most.

In the lower part of the top section of a profile in Sales Navigator, you'll find tabs that include About, Relationship, Experience, and CRM (CRM only shows up if relevant with an Advanced Plus subscription). The Relationship feature in Sales Navigator offers three helpful suggestions for personalizing your outreach and engaging with potential leads:

Recent activity on LinkedIn: This section allows you to quickly view the lead's recent activity on LinkedIn, providing you insights into what is currently top of mind for them and suggesting material you can reference in your outreach.

What you share in common: This area gives you a summary of any shared connections, LinkedIn groups, past employers, or education you have in common with the individual. This can provide an easy way to establish common ground and build rapport in your outreach.

Get introduced: In this section, Sales Navigator provides you with a list of connections you share with the individual who may be able to provide you with a warm introduction within your or your company's network. This is especially useful if you have access to TeamLink, which allows you to leverage the power of your entire company's network to identify potential introductions.

Another powerful feature you'll see when viewing a leads profile in Sales Navigator is "Similar leads at (company name)." It suggests other people within the same organization you may want to reach out to. This is particularly helpful for account research. By using this feature, you can ask your lead if one or more specific individuals (based on your research) should be included at the next meeting. For example, during a discovery meeting, you can ask, "Should [NAME], the [TITLE], be part of our next meeting?" This approach shows that you've invested time in understanding the company's organizational structure and individuals, even if you don't get a direct answer to your question.

Get Relevant Account Updates and Alerts

With LinkedIn's Sales Navigator, you can receive relevant updates and alerts for your saved companies (Accounts) and contacts (Leads). Utilize the filters to personalize your feed, making it easier to stay updated on the accounts and individuals you're targeting and wanting to build relationships with, without the need to sift through endless content and updates.

In Sales Navigator's home tab, you can modify your newsfeed by filtering updates from those who've changed jobs, leads who are featured in the news, those sharing content, and updates about your saved accounts. Each filter grants you the opportunity to engage with your lead or key account more effectively. This feature aids you in determining the most beneficial filters for each account or contact.

If you work for a company, I also recommend saving your own company and your competitors as leads and accounts to stay on top of changes and trends in your industry. This can help you stay informed about what's on the mind of your company's top executives, colleagues, and competitors.

Sales Navigator Settings

You can further personalize your experience in Sales Navigator by customizing your settings. To access your settings page, click on your image in the top-right corner of the page and select "Settings."

Settings

Upgrade your plan

Sales Navigator Coach

Referrals

Who's Viewed Your Profile

Social Selling Index

User agreement

Privacy policy

Cookie policy

Go to LinkedIn.com

Log out

Sales Navigator provides alerts when a saved lead or contact at a saved account views your profile. It also has its own settings page, where you can control how much information about yourself others can see when you visit their profile.

It's important to note that the settings on LinkedIn and Sales Navigator are separate. Unless there's a specific need for anonymity, allowing people to see when you've viewed their profile can increase their awareness of you and boost the likelihood of engagement—particularly if they often check profile viewers before engaging. Sales Navigator's "Alerts" feature keeps you informed about your saved leads and accounts, giving you alerts related to their activities and suggesting next steps. These can be a useful engagement trigger.

Account alert preferences include:

- Account Growth
- Buyer Intent
- New Decision Makers
- Account News
- Account Updates
- Suggested Leads
- Account Risk

Lead alert preferences include:

- Career Changes
- Lead Engagement
- Lead News
- Lead Shares
- Suggested Leads

By activating these alerts, you can stay updated on the most relevant accounts and leads and initiate proactive engagement.

If you are using the free version of LinkedIn or have a Premium Business subscription, theseare the action steps for you to take now:

Step 1: Familiarize Yourself with LinkedIn's Advanced Search: Start using LinkedIn's Advanced Search feature. Practice using various search filters like location, industry, and job function.

Step 2: Incorporate Boolean Searches: Apply Boolean search operators such as AND, OR, and NOT to refine your search results. Experiment with these operators to enhance the quality of your search results.

Step 3: Leverage Alumni Networks: If relevant, use the LinkedIn alumni function to locate and network with alumni from your school who may be potential clients. Remember to personalize your connection requests.

Step 4: Conduct Prospect Research: Deep-dive into LinkedIn profiles of potential clients to gather relevant information about their professional needs and challenges. Take note of their connections, interests, and overall activity on LinkedIn.

Step 5: Identify High-Potential Clients: Use your acquired knowledge to start building a list of high-potential clients on LinkedIn.

The process of finding and engaging potential clients is dynamic and continuous. Keep refining your strategy based on the responses and changes you observe in potential clients' profiles and activities.

If you are using Sales Navigator, here are the steps to put what you've learned into action:

Step 1: Create Your Lead Lists: Start by creating your lead lists in Sales Navigator to manage your leads. Begin saving leads into relevant lead lists to keep your prospects organized and readily accessible.

Step 2: Develop Buyer Personas: Create buyer personas to target your potential clients more easily when you are doing searches on Sales Navigator.

Step 3: Establish Saved Searches for Leads: Utilize the "Save search" feature in Sales Navigator for your leads. By creating one or more saved searches based on specific criteria that match your ideal client personas, you can ensure that you're consistently finding the most relevant leads.

Step 4: Create Saved Searches for Accounts (if relevant): If you're also targeting specific companies, create saved searches for accounts. Similar to leads, this can help you stay updated on company updates and changes that may present new opportunities.

Step 5: Set Up Relevant Alerts: Define and set up your alerts in Sales Navigator. This could include alerts for account growth, new decision makers, lead engagement, etc. The goal here is to receive timely updates on the accounts and leads that matter most to you.

As you put these steps into action, remember to fully leverage the "Spotlights" feature in Sales Navigator. It provides valuable insights about your leads and accounts, allowing you to better customize your outreach and engagement efforts.

Keep in mind, proficiency with Sales Navigator comes with practice. Continually refine your approach based on the responses and changes you observe in your ideal clients' behavior. By effectively leveraging these tools and features, you'll be well-equipped to increase your lead generation productivity and enhance your engagement strategy with your prospects.

CHAPTER SEVEN

Convert Connections to Clients with The LINK Method™

I can't tell you how many LinkedIn and social selling experts I've heard say that the key to success is through sharing content.

I disagree!

Content has its role, and it's an important one I discuss in depth in the next two chapters; but content alone is not going to generate a steady stream of new clients, not one that is predictable. What will is a direct outreach to targeted prospects, which is the fastest, most reliable, and most effective way to generate leads and clients on LinkedIn when done right.

Many of my clients, and the students I've taught through my workshops and online training programs, expressed a similar challenge before working with me. They didn't know what to do after the initial connection request. They had a lot of questions, such as:

- So, we've connected; now what?
- What do I say in a message?
- How do I send a message without coming across as spammy?
- What are the steps I need to follow and in what time frame?

This is precisely why I created a method and broke it down into a simple system to show you exactly what to do, what to say, and when to do it. The

LINK Method™ is a system of sending a sequence of messages to a prospect that starts with connecting with them on LinkedIn and moves to an offline conversation. In order to effectively use this method, you must incorporate personalization into everything you do.

The Importance of Personalization

Your prospects want to be heard, understood, remembered, and respected. Failing to meet these expectations will place you in the bracket of just another person attempting to make a sale. This could result in them seeking solutions elsewhere with someone who truly gets them. To drive home this point, imagine you are the lead—wouldn't you prefer someone who takes the time to understand your unique needs and challenges?

Remember, although you may be selling to a company, your primary focus should be on establishing rapport with the individuals making the decisions. These individuals have specific needs and challenges, and building personal connections with them is critical for them to feel you genuinely care about resolving their problems.

The LINK Method™

To personalize your approach effectively and nurture meaningful relationships with your leads, let me introduce The LINK Method™. This method serves as a guide to go from a connection request to a booked appointment, paving the way for you to become a champion LinkedIn connection and relationship builder. For each step in this sequence, I'll help you understand the objective and timing, and learn how to structure each message.

In targeting elusive individuals, particularly high-level executives in larger corporations or well-known influencers, many may be wary about accepting connection requests from strangers. As I mentioned in an earlier chapter, a recommended strategy would be to first follow them and interact with their content if they are active on LinkedIn. A thoughtful comment here and there will increase the chances of them recognizing you when you send a connection request. If they aren't posting on LinkedIn, consider conducting a Google/Bing search for any insights or details about them, or check if they're active on other social platforms.

Once you've confirmed your prospect's presence on LinkedIn and are ready to engage, prioritize initiating authentic, personalized conversations that put their needs first. Selling comes later. Like any meaningful relationship, trust and rapport take time to build.

Now let's dive into the details of The LINK Method™, providing practical tips and strategies to create messages that elicit a response within each of its five steps.

The LINK Method™

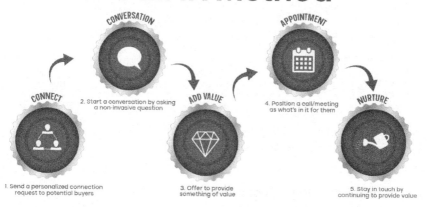

1. Send a personalized connection request to potential buyers

2. Start a conversation by asking a non-invasive question

3. Offer to provide something of value

4. Position a call/meeting as what's in it for them

5. Stay in touch by continuing to provide value

Step 1: Connect

The initial connection request on LinkedIn is a crucial step. To make a positive impression, personalization is key. This requires reviewing the person's profile before reaching out to identify something you can reference in your message. Your personalized connection request can reference a shared experience or interest, comment on a recent post they made, congratulate them on an accomplishment, compliment their organization, or mention a mutual connection who has given you permission to use their name.

To differentiate yourself from others also using LinkedIn for lead generation, ensure your message answers the question they're likely asking themselves when they receive a connection request from a complete stranger— "Who is this person, and why are they trying to connect with me?" —in 300 characters or fewer.

Also, if you've met potential clients in the past and are not connected to them on LinkedIn, send them a connection request reminding them of how or when you met.

GOAL: Get them to accept your connection request. Answer the question they have: who is this person, and why do they want to connect with me?

OBJECTIVE: Keep it simple, make it all about them, and make sure it's personalized.

TIMING: Send the connection request right after determining that the individual is a prospect. However, in the case of high-level executives or influencers, consider engaging with their LinkedIn posts for a while before sending a request, to build some familiarity.

Structuring your Step 1 connection request:

When crafting your connection request message, consider using one of these approaches:

- Highlight commonalities such as alumni status, shared interests, volunteer activities, or previous employers.
- Refer to their recent LinkedIn posts.

- Offer congratulations on recent achievements or recognitions.
- Provide a positive remark about their company.
- Mention a mutual connection who has allowed you to use their name.

Step 2: Conversation

After your connection request is accepted, the next crucial step is to initiate a conversation. The aim is not to sell anything at this point, but to start a dialogue, ideally by asking a question that prompts a response.

GOAL: Establish a friendly dialogue and two-way communication.

OBJECTIVE: Keep the conversation light and non-invasive. The question you pose should be answerable within 30 seconds. It doesn't necessarily have to be business-related; the primary purpose is to facilitate quick, comfortable two-way communication.

TIMING: Ideally, this message should be sent approximately 3–5 days after they have accepted your connection request.

Structuring your Step 2 message to initiate a conversation:

Keep it simple:

- Start by expressing gratitude for their acceptance of your connection request.
- Ask them a question they can answer in 30 seconds or less; if it takes longer, they will likely ignore it.
- You must ensure the question you are asking in no way feels invasive.
- Imagine that you met this individual at an in-person event; how would you spark up a conversation?

This message will be ten times more effective when you've taken the time to truly personalize it. Here are some ideas to help you determine the best question to ask:

- If they have shared something recently on LinkedIn, consider asking a question related to the topic they shared.
- Ask them about an interest or cause mentioned in their profile.
- Reference a recent announcement from their company.
- If the above suggestions don't fit, consider asking their opinion on a trending topic within their industry.

It's important to note that this step of starting a conversation is essential, because you want to create a two-way dialogue in your LinkedIn message thread. If your messages only show up one after another with no interaction on their part, they will be more likely to ignore your future messages, or even remove you as a connection.

If your prospect responds to your message, it's important to reply with a short and respectful response and leave it there for now. This will position you well for the next message you'll send them.

Step 3: Add Value

The next message you want to send should provide value. Your goal is to position yourself and your company as highly knowledgeable about their industry and/or their specific role responsibilities. To accomplish this, you need a profound understanding of their industry and key issues. You can then offer a content resource that aligns with these insights.

Remember, the content you provide should not be promotional. It must offer genuine insights and address the questions or challenges they may have. It could be created by you, your company, or even industry authorities. The form it takes can also vary. Videos, infographics, or interactive content might be more engaging for some types of individuals; however, traditional text-based articles or white papers work particularly well in this step.

When deciding what content to share, you must consider these questions:

- What are they interested in or focused on based on their role?
- What are the hot topics in their industry?
- What problems or challenges is their industry facing?
- What direction is their company or industry moving toward?
- What are the challenges their CEO has disclosed in the company's public disclosure (if applicable)?

Another point to consider is the most common personality type associated with various roles. This will help you in determining the best format of content to use. As an example, if you are targeting creative roles, they will often prefer visual content, whereas technical roles will appreciate in-depth text-based research. This comes down to knowing your target market. I'll share more on how to create content for this step in the next two chapters.

GOAL: Add value, usually with a content resource.

OBJECTIVE: Keep your message concise and ensure it is tailored to them, relevant to their role and industry, and offers value—remember, value from their perspective, not yours.

TIMING: Send this message approximately two weeks (or longer) after message two.

Structuring your Step 3 message to add value:

When offering the content, keep it simple and follow these guidelines:

- Start with a polite and professional opening. Mention that you were thinking about their company or something related to their specific role.

- Identify a goal, objective, problem, or challenge that is relevant to their company, or something for which they are responsible.
- Reference the type of content (e.g., article, white paper, video) and its title, making sure it's relevant to their industry and role. Include one to two benefits they will get from reviewing that content.
- End by asking if they would be interested in receiving it.

> **FOR EXAMPLE:** Hi [Name], I was thinking of [name of their company] and [goal/objective/problem/challenge—something highly relatable to their company or something they are accountable for in their role]. I thought you would find value in [title and type of content piece] because it highlights [benefit 1] and [benefit 2] to [their industry/role]. Would this interest you? If so, I'd be happy to send it to you.

It's crucial to ask your prospect if they would be interested in the content, rather than just directly sending a link. This is a more respectful approach, and they are more likely to engage with the content. If you have a Sales Navigator Advanced or Advanced Plus subscription, consider using Smart Links to track engagement, which lets you see if and for how long the prospect accessed the content. Otherwise my preferred method for delivering a piece of content in this step is in the form of a PDF after they have expressed interest in receiving it.

Step 4: Book Appointment

The aim of converting a prospect into a client requires moving the conversation offline and booking an appointment. Only then can you engage in a sales conversation. This message will be geared toward achieving this goal.

If the prospect did not respond to your Step 3 message, it's important to acknowledge this respectfully in this message.

Structuring your Step 4 message to book an appointment:

Keep it simple:

- Start with a reference to a previous conversation (if relevant) to establish a friendly and personal tone.
- Ask them if they found value in the content you sent them in the last message. If you didn't send it because they didn't respond, acknowledge this in the message.
- Explain that you have an idea or something helpful that you think would be worth their time for an introductory conversation.
- Clearly identify what's in it for them from their perspective, not yours.
- Assure them that the conversation will be brief, with the possibility of scheduling a more detailed discussion later if it's worthwhile to them.
- Ask if there's someone else in their company who might be a better fit for this conversation if they're not the appropriate contact.
- Inquire if there is a convenient day/time for them in the next week to have this conversation. If they are a C-suite executive, consider asking if there is an executive assistant, business manager, or chief of staff you could work with to coordinate a time.

Remember, your message should assure the prospect that their time will be well spent and offer tangible benefits such as ideas for cost savings, revenue increase, improved efficiencies, competitive advantage, or innovation.

The key is to make the message short, direct, and focused on the prospect's needs. Respecting their time and demonstrating your value increases their likelihood of agreeing to an appointment.

Step 5: Nurture

The aim of this step is to keep building the relationship with your prospects, who may not be ready to commit to a purchase. Regular and meaningful engagement on LinkedIn can help keep you top-of-mind while establishing you as an authority in their mind.

GOAL: Nurture the relationship.

OBJECTIVE: The timing of your initial outreach may not have aligned with the prospect's readiness to engage or make a purchase. The objective is to stay in touch by continuing to add value, thereby creating opportunities to reinitiate direct contact like a phone call when the time is right for them.

TIMING: Send a nurturing message 2–3 months after the last contact, and then quarterly to remain on their radar.

Structuring your Step 5 nurturing messages:

Use these strategies for nurturing relationships with prospects. These strategies are designed to engage and add value to your interactions, deepening your connection with potential and existing clients.

Engagement Strategies

- **Relevance:** Make sure all your communication, content, and interactions align with the individual and their company. This shows respect for their time and a commitment to providing useful information.
- **Personalization:** Tailor your interactions to what you know about the individual. If they've been promoted, started a new project, or received recognition, acknowledge it. This signals your investment in the relationship beyond making a sale.
- **Engagement:** Regularly like, comment on and, when appropriate, share your connections' posts. This enhances your visibility and indicates your genuine interest.

Content Strategies

- **Continue to add value:** Reference a goal, objective, problem, or challenge they are likely facing, and provide relevant content to address it, similar to your Step 3 message.
- **News and industry trends:** Share major developments or trends in their industry to provide value and showcase your knowledge and dedication to their sector.

Outreach Strategies

- **Regular check-ins:** Touch base with them occasionally without an agenda. Asking how they're doing or if they need anything can be a powerful relationship-building tool.
- **Events and webinars:** Invite them to relevant webinars, conferences, or other events. The invitation itself demonstrates thoughtfulness, even if they choose not to attend.

By maintaining a balance of personalized engagement, value-added content, and genuine relationship building, you'll increase the likelihood of transforming a prospect into a loyal client.

Remember, nurturing relationships is not a one-size-fits-all process—it requires understanding, care, and a commitment to value.

To recap, the five steps in The LINK Method™ are:

Step 1: Connect—Send a personalized connection request to prospects.

Step 2: Conversation—Start a conversation by asking a non-invasive question.

Step 3: Add Value—Offer something of value that aligns with their industry or role.

Step 4: Book Appointment—Position a call or meeting in terms of the benefits they will gain.

Step 5: Nurture—Stay engaged and continually provide value, keeping you at the forefront of their minds for future business opportunities.

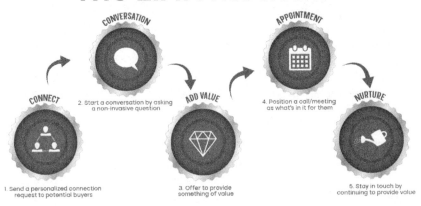

Regular and authentic interaction with their posts on LinkedIn and other social media platforms, combined with an awareness of alerts you receive on LinkedIn or Sales Navigator, provides a multitude of opportunities for meaningful engagement.

Alerts That Provide Natural Engagement Opportunities

In addition to the messages you send as part of The LINK Method™, there will likely be numerous other opportunities to engage with or send messages to your connections. These "trigger events" provide natural opportunities to interact with your connections, helping you build and nurture relationships with prospects.

Below are common alerts you will receive that provide natural engagement opportunities:

- Job change within the past 90 days
- Promotion
- They or their company were mentioned in the news
- They've recently posted something on LinkedIn
- They engage with your Smart Links content
- They shared an accomplishment or milestone on LinkedIn

In every engagement, ensure that your interaction is relevant to the person or situation. The objective is to stay on their radar, offer value, build trust, and eventually become the go-to person when they require the solution you offer. By being strategic and thoughtful in your interactions, you're building a strong, lasting relationship that may lead to future business opportunities.

Warm Introductions and Referrals

Your existing network is an invaluable resource with the potential to significantly contribute to your sales. Establishing relationships with those who trust you enough to introduce you to their own connections can be an impactful way to tap into this resource. A recent LinkedIn survey revealed that buyers are five times more likely to engage via a warm referral, and that 84% of B2B decision-makers initiate their buying process with a referral.

Yet, requesting an introduction requires a thoughtful approach to avoid damaging existing relationships. Remember, you are requesting a favor. Be respectful and express your gratitude, irrespective of the response.

Crafting the message for your request is crucial, and addressing these key points can increase its effectiveness:

1. Establish a personal connection in your initial sentence.
2. Ask if they're acquainted well enough with the prospect to provide an introduction.
3. Assure them you'll provide the introductory message to make it quick and easy for them.
4. Express gratitude for their time and consideration.

EXAMPLE: Hello [Name], I hope you've had a nice summer. I noticed you're connected with [Name of prospect + LinkedIn URL], and I would love to speak with them about [briefly explain why you want to speak with them]. Do you happen to know them well enough to provide an introduction? I can provide the message to send, so it's as easy as possible for you. Thank you for your time, and I appreciate any help you can provide.

If They Decline or Aren't Well-Acquainted with the Prospect

Respond with a polite message thanking them for their time and consideration. It's vital to maintain the relationship for future opportunities. Remember, relationship-building is a long-term strategy, and not every connection will yield immediate results.

If They Agree to Provide an Introduction: Follow-up Message

If your connection accepts your request, follow up promptly. Thank them, provide a concise sample message they can use, and make the process as effortless as possible for them. This increases the likelihood of them following through. Your follow-up should include:

- Gratitude for their willingness to introduce you.
- A simple and concise message they can copy and paste.
- Mention of the shared connection or interest for added credibility.
- Clear communication of the introduction's purpose and desired outcome.
- Encouragement for the referred person to connect, including your contact details.

Here's an example follow-up message that includes the five important points:

Hi [Contact], thank you for agreeing to introduce me to [Name]. Your help is greatly appreciated.

To make it as easy as possible for you, here's a sample message you can send:

"Hi [Name], I wanted to introduce you to [your name], who I think you would find value in speaking with. [Your name] is an expert in [insert your area of expertise or industry], and I believe there may be some valuable synergies between your work and theirs. Do you have time this week to connect with [your name]?"

Thank you again for your help with this introduction.

[Your Name]

By following the best practices outlined here, you can effectively leverage your network for warm introductions and referrals. Always show appreciation, simplify the process for your contacts, and offer value in return. This will help you build robust relationships and enhance your chances of social selling success.

10 Best Practices for Increasing Message Response Rates

Here are some key practices that can boost the response rates to your LinkedIn messages:

- **Emphasize quality over quantity:** Avoid overwhelming recipients with excessive messages. Send a follow-up only after an appropriate duration as stated in the timing of each of the five steps of The LINK Method™. Also, avoid repeating the same message.

- **Be concise:** Keep your messages polite, brief, and clear. Often, less is more.

- **Personalize your messages:** Tailor every message to the recipient to make them feel seen and valued.

- **Focus on their needs:** Concentrate on the recipient's needs, interests, and goals rather than your solution.

- **Create a clear call to action:** Indicate clearly what the desired next step is.

- **Combine LinkedIn outreach with other channels:** Although LinkedIn can generate higher response rates than emails or cold calls, it's advisable to diversify your communication channels to determine the most effective approach.

- **Choose recipients wisely:** Active LinkedIn users with complete profiles, a large network, and regular updates tend to respond more frequently.

- **Utilize mutual connections:** Take advantage of your network to get introduced, but remember that just because someone is connected to someone on LinkedIn, it doesn't mean they know them. Always ask this first.
- **Enhance your professional profile:** An unimpressive profile can discourage responses. Ensure your profile showcases your credibility and value.
- **Leverage commonalities:** When possible, approach leads with whom you share something in common. LinkedIn states that individuals are 46% more likely to receive a response when reaching out to leads with shared interests or experiences.

By following these best practices, you can optimize your outreach and significantly increase your response rates on LinkedIn.

Handling a Lack of Response

Even with the best-executed messages, it's not possible to get a response from every person you reach out to. Sales is, after all, a numbers game, and there are several reasons why your messages may not resonate with every prospect. They could be:

- Not within your target market
- Uninterested in your offering at present
- Not prepared for the solution you offer
- Currently prioritizing other aspects
- Distracted by personal or professional issues
- Unengaged by your message, suggesting a need for revision
- Not the appropriate contact for your outreach

However, this does not exclude them from a potential interest in the future. Persistence and keeping yourself top of mind are key. Don't let non-responsiveness deter you from consistently adding value and nurturing the relationship.

If you're experiencing low response rates, it's time to:

- Revisit your message strategy and re-write your messages, if necessary
- Refine your targeting to focus on a more specific audience
- Experiment with different contact methods like email or phone
- Offer a different type of value to pique the prospect's interest
- Continue to nurture the relationship, staying relevant by sharing meaningful content and actively engaging with their LinkedIn activities.

To sum up, The LINK Method™ provides a detailed roadmap for effectively using LinkedIn and Sales Navigator to connect with prospects, build relationships, and convert leads into clients. The LINK Method's five steps enable you to build rapport, contribute value, and position yourself as a trusted authority on your topic. Regular engagement and monitoring of trigger events can also help nurture relationships and increase the likelihood of future business opportunities. This methodical approach will allow you to tap into the full potential of lead generation on LinkedIn.

Remember, while the examples provided here serve as a useful guide, each message should be uniquely tailored to the specific individual, their company, and their industry. Any responses they've sent should also be considered while composing future messages. Personalization and authenticity are critical to build strong relationships with prospects on LinkedIn, so invest the time in customizing each message.

Start integrating the techniques outlined in this chapter into your LinkedIn strategy to build relationships and nurture prospects effectively:

Step 1: Craft Messages for Prospects: Use LinkedIn or Sales Navigator to identify three good prospects who closely match your ideal client profile. For each one, prepare a personalized sequence of the first four messages in accordance with The LINK Method™.

Step 2: Engage Using Alerts: Review your notifications on LinkedIn, or if you are using Sales Navigator look through the "Alerts" section for your saved leads. Pick five potential clients with recent updates or activities that can serve as natural touchpoints for engagement. Compose personalized, thoughtful messages or comments in response to these alerts, further strengthening the relationship.

Step 3: Reconnect with Dormant Leads: Identify prospects within your connections that you've not interacted with for some time. Create a nurturing message to re-engage with these individuals, offering them something of value.

If you're not seeing the desired level of responses, refer to this chapter's section on "Best Practices for Increasing Message Response Rates" and "Handling a Lack of Response." By continuously evaluating and refining your approach, you can incrementally improve your social selling strategy and results.

PART THREE

EXECUTION

CHAPTER EIGHT

Impactful Content to Increase Reach and Influence

LinkedIn is not just a professional platform—it's a dynamic meeting place for businesses, professionals, and industry leaders. It provides the opportunity to connect with peers, build relationships with prospects, and establish your position as an authority in your field.

To make this possible, the content you share should resonate with your audience, enrich their professional journeys, and enhance your credibility. By sharing enlightening and engaging content, you demonstrate your knowledge and expertise, helping to build trust and authority within your network and the prospects you are connecting with on LinkedIn.

Throughout this chapter, I'll unpack the fundamental components of effective content and offer tips for crafting various content types. I'll discuss the range of topics to post on LinkedIn to stir interest and stimulate engagement. However, before I delve into those details, it's crucial to understand what LinkedIn's algorithm seeks and how it prioritizes content.

Understanding LinkedIn's Algorithm

It's vital to understand LinkedIn's algorithm to maximize the reach and engagement of each post you share. The current LinkedIn algorithm prioritizes knowledge and insightful advice, to emphasize professionalism and quality over quantity instead of viral content.

LinkedIn encourages users to build a community around content that showcases their unique expertise. The platform identifies "knowledge and advice" through several metrics:

- **Relevance to a specific audience**: Every post is assessed for its relevance to a specific audience. LinkedIn's algorithm identifies who might find a post relevant, ensuring the content reaches the right audience. For example, a post about B2B marketing will be shared with individuals in that sector. The key for you is to share knowledge to help your target audience.

- **Expertise of the author:** LinkedIn also evaluates the author's authority and expertise on the topic they're posting about. The author's credibility is a crucial determinant in evaluating the post's value. LinkedIn's algorithm will recognize this and limit the reach of your post if you're posting about a topic you have no background in.

- **Quality of comments:** Unlike other platforms that reward posts with a high number of comments, LinkedIn focuses on the quality of the comments. Posts with meaningful comments that contribute to a discussion are more likely to be promoted by the algorithm.

- **Unique Perspective**: LinkedIn's algorithm also considers whether a post provides a unique perspective or insight rather than generic information. Posts that offer personal insights or opinions are more likely to be promoted organically by LinkedIn.

Master LinkedIn's Algorithm with Tips for Every Influencing Factor

When it comes to crafting LinkedIn posts, aim to share compelling content that will captivate your target audience. The following tips will guide you in creating or curating more effective content that aligns with LinkedIn's algorithm preferences.

Know your audience: Consider your ideal audience before posting. The LinkedIn algorithm prioritizes content that resonates with a specific audience. Make sure your content addresses the needs, questions, or interests of your connections and followers.

Share expert knowledge: LinkedIn values content that offers valuable insights and advice. Leverage your industry expertise and share knowledge that positions you as a professional in your field. This helps establish authority and boosts the visibility of your LinkedIn posts.

Stick to your expertise: LinkedIn assesses whether the authors of posts are authorities on the subjects they've posted about. To build credibility and improve your content visibility, focus on topics within your industry or areas of expertise.

Encourage meaningful engagement: LinkedIn's algorithm values meaningful comments. To encourage substantive responses from your audience, ask open-ended questions, initiate thought-provoking discussions, or share interesting industry perspectives.

Be consistent: Regular posting increases the likelihood that your followers will see your content. It also signals to LinkedIn's algorithm that you're an active user. Strive for a consistent posting schedule that keeps your content visible and engaging.

Incorporate personal insights: Content that includes personalized insights tends to gain more traction. Go beyond generic information to include your unique perspectives and insights, which LinkedIn's algorithm appreciates.

Engage with comments: Engage with individuals who comment on your posts. This encourages further interaction and is also viewed favorably by LinkedIn's algorithm, increasing your post's visibility.

Experiment with content formats: LinkedIn supports various content types, including text, images, videos, and documents. Try different formats to see which one resonates most with your audience and achieves the highest engagement.

Prioritize targeted reach: While the idea of reaching a broad audience can be appealing, LinkedIn has moved away from rewarding virality. Instead, focus on creating valuable, insightful content that resonates with the right people. This approach is more likely to drive meaningful engagement and build valuable connections.

Leverage unspoken metrics: While LinkedIn hasn't publicly confirmed this, my observations suggest that there are two "unspoken metrics" that can significantly boost your content's reach. First, the "...see more" clicks, or the number of times people click to expand and read your entire post. This signals that your initial lines have successfully captured attention. Second, the time spent on your post; the longer someone lingers, the more valuable the content appears to be in LinkedIn's eyes. That's why utilizing up to 3,000 characters can be beneficial; it keeps readers engaged for longer, which in turn prompts LinkedIn to show your post to a broader audience.

Understanding LinkedIn's algorithm offers a significant advantage in navigating the platform effectively. By implementing these strategies, you can align your content creation efforts with what LinkedIn values—authenticity, expertise, and meaningful engagement. This knowledge empowers you to share content that not only resonates with your target audience but also maximizes visibility, ultimately amplifying your professional presence and impact on LinkedIn.

Combining Content Curation and Creation

Boosting your professional visibility on LinkedIn requires sharing content that is both relevant and engaging for your target audience. Achieving a balance between content curation, creation, and use of AI ensures a constant flow of diverse and valuable posts. Here's how you can utilize various types of content:

- **LinkedIn posts:** Regularly share insights, industry news, or updates relevant to your audience. These can be your own thoughts or ideas, or excerpts from larger pieces of content. Making your posts interactive by asking questions or seeking opinions can also drive engagement.
- **Shared articles/links:** Curate and share articles, blog posts, or news stories from reputable sources your audience would find interesting and useful. Don't just share the link—add your perspective or key takeaways to make it more engaging.
- **LinkedIn articles and newsletters:** Build your authority by creating longer-form content such as articles or newsletters. These can combine industry news and trends with your original content to keep your audience informed and engaged.
- **Visual content:** Use infographics, images, or videos to deliver information in an appealing way. Visuals are highly shareable and can enhance audience engagement. Short, focused videos that showcase your expertise or offer insights into your ideal client's challenges can be particularly effective.

- **Document/carousel posts:** Document posts allow you to upload multi-page documents, reports, whitepapers, eBooks, and slide decks directly to your LinkedIn feed. Readers can easily flip through your document by swiping or using on-screen controls. You can also create an eye-catching carousel preview of your document to promote clicks and views. Document posts are ideal for showcasing research, how-to guides, case studies, and other long-form marketing content. Include a strong headline and description to highlight key insights, takeaways, and calls to action. Add visual interest with cover images, graphics, quotes, and charts throughout your document.

- **Reposts:** Sharing valuable insights, discussions, or news through reposting on LinkedIn is an effective strategy for engaging your target audience. It's important to remember that when you repost you're endorsing the perspective shared by the original author of the post. Instead of simply pressing "repost," enrich the repost by adding your unique viewpoint or analysis.

- **Polls:** Kick-start conversations and encourage engagement with polls. Use them to gather insights from your audience or ask for their opinions on relevant topics.

- **AI tools:** Utilize AI tools to inspire ideas for new posts. Large language models (LLMs) can assist in identifying trending topics within your industry or areas of interest, and suggest content ideas that will resonate with your audience. This way, you ensure your posts stay relevant and engaging, further increasing your visibility and credibility on the platform.

The key to creating compelling content lies in storytelling. Regardless of the format, incorporate personal anecdotes, case studies, or examples to emphasize your points and make your content more memorable. This way, you engage your audience on a deeper, more personal level, building stronger connections.

Essential Tips for Incorporating Storytelling into Your Content

- **Identify the core message:** Know the central idea you want to convey.

- **Speak to your target market:** Tailor the story to resonate with your target demographic.

- **Create an emotional connection:** Use characters or situations your reader can relate to.

- **Conflict and resolution:** Introduce a problem early in your story to grab the reader's attention, then guide them through how that problem gets solved. This creates a journey that keeps the reader interested from start to finish.

- **Use vivid imagery:** Use descriptive words and details to paint a vivid picture in the reader's mind. This makes the story much more engaging.

- **Pacing is key:** Control the rhythm and flow to maintain audience interest without rushing or dragging the story.

- **Review and refine:** Tighten the narrative by removing unnecessary details.

Remember to maintain a balance between content curation, creation, and AI utilization. While curation can help share valuable information and build engagement, combining this with original content and insights derived from AI will help demonstrate your unique perspective and expertise. This mixed approach aids in positioning you as a valuable source of information and insight.

Leverage the Power of Generative AI Tools

If you're looking to elevate your LinkedIn presence, you know it calls for the regular production of compelling content. The challenge, however, is that writing unique, engaging content can be time-consuming. The good news is that generative AI tools like ChatGPT, Bing Chat, Claude-2, and Google Bard have evolved to simplify the process.

These AI tools are powerful language models that utilize deep learning to generate human-like text. They can provide content ideas, aid in research, and even assist in crafting your content. Here's how AI tools can supercharge your content creation for LinkedIn:

- **Content ideation:** Struggling with writer's block? AI can generate endless ideas for content, including LinkedIn posts or articles.
- **Research:** AI can quickly gather relevant and credible sources for your content, saving you valuable time.
- **Writing assistance:** AI tools can enhance your writing style. Input a sentence or a paragraph, and let AI suggest improvements and fix any grammatical errors. This results in polished, professional-grade copy.

Here are a couple of examples of AI prompts you can use:

FOR IDEATION: You are an expert at generating interesting, engaging, and educational content. Provide me with 10 bite-sized (micro) content ideas that would be of interest to [TARGET AUDIENCE]. I want topics that are top-of-mind issues for [INDUSTRY].

FOR CONTENT CREATION: You are a content marketing expert. Help me create an engaging and insightful post for [TARGET MARKET] on [TOPIC] to help them [DESIRE/GOAL/SOLVE PROBLEM]. The post should intrigue and inform, leaving the readers not only educated but inspired to act. Limit it to under 3,000 characters and use a friendly and engaging tone. Begin with a sentence that captures their attention, and keep the sentences and paragraphs short with a reader-friendly layout.

While AI tools like ChatGPT are powerful allies in content creation, it's essential to remember that they complement, not replace, human creativity and critical thinking. These tools streamline your content creation process, making it more efficient, while you retain the critical role of infusing your personal insights and expertise by editing the AI content.

If the transformative power of AI intrigues you, there's much more to explore, especially when it comes to using generative AI for content creation, sales, and marketing. There is so much to explore that I've dedicated my next book entirely to this topic, ***Supercharged: Ignite Your Sales and Marketing with Artificial Intelligence***.

In the next chapter, I'll share some specific strategies for crafting effective prompts that enable AI to assist you in generating high-quality content.

Additionally, I've included bonus prompts in the "LinkedIn Unlocked: Resource Pack" to give you a jumpstart in creating compelling content through AI. This resource is available for download at **LinkedinUnlockedBook.com** by using the secret word ***Bonus***.

The future of content creation is here, and it's powered by AI. Don't wait to start exploring the endless possibilities this technology has to offer.

Sharing Impactful Content on LinkedIn

Your posts play a vital role in building your personal brand and establishing credibility on LinkedIn. But how can you consistently create posts that engage your audience and spark meaningful conversations? Here's a guide to help you do just that.

Finding content ideas: Identifying what your target audience is interested in is the starting point for generating content ideas. Ask yourself what questions they might have. What challenges are they facing? How can your own experiences and expertise provide solutions or insights?

AI tools, like ChatGPT, can prove incredibly useful in this process, generating numerous content ideas based on the parameters you set. In addition to AI, look at LinkedIn's newsfeed, and search for posts by keywords and topics to find relevant articles and posts that can inspire your own content.

Structuring LinkedIn posts for maximum impact: Crafting a compelling LinkedIn post involves strategic structure and elements. Here are the crucial ones:

- **Attention-grabbing opening or hook**: Begin your post with an interesting statement or question that piques the interest of your audience. Make them want to click "...see more" to continue reading.
- **Clear, concise content**: Use short paragraphs and bullet points for clarity and readability. This makes it easier for your audience to quickly digest your message and more likely they will read it.
- **Visual elements**: Occasionally incorporate relevant images, documents/carousels, or videos to make your post more visually appealing and engaging. Use images and infographics to make your posts more sharable.
- **Call to action**: Close your post with a CTA to spur audience engagement, encouraging them to comment on your content. You can ask a question, invite opinions, or simply ask them if they found your post valuable.

Optimizing with AI: Once you've drafted your post, use AI tools like ChatGPT to review and refine your copy. It can provide suggestions to improve your writing and correct your grammar to ensure a polished and professional looking post.

Remember, your goal is to create content that resonates with your audience's needs and challenges, showcasing your expertise in the process.

Crafting High-Impact LinkedIn Posts: Your Comprehensive Checklist

The magic of a high-impact LinkedIn post lies in the details—how you craft that post can make all the difference between it getting lost in the feed or increasing your reach and influence. To help you master this art, I've created a comprehensive checklist that will guide you through each step of creating a LinkedIn post that is both valuable and impactful.

LINKEDIN POST CHECKLIST
☐ Does the post focus on a subject matter where you possess demonstrable expertise or unique insights?
☐ Have you crafted a captivating lead sentence that instantly draws readers in?
☐ Does the content offer value by being informative, motivational, or educational to your audience?
☐ Is your core message presented clearly and concisely?
☐ Does your post present an idea that either sparks curiosity or is actionable for your audience?
☐ Are your sentences short?
☐ Have you utilized white space to make your post more scannable and reader-friendly?
☐ Is everything easy to understand and written in straightforward language?
☐ Have you written in conversational language that invites reader engagement?
☐ Perform a read-aloud test: Does the post sound as though it's coming from a real person?
☐ Have you incorporated relevant emojis to add personality to your text?

☐	Could your post benefit from a document or carousel to enrich content and capture greater attention?
☐	Have you concluded with a call-to-action that encourages reader interaction or next steps?
☐	Have you proofread for typos, grammatical errors, and inconsistencies before posting?
☐	When appropriate, have you tagged relevant individuals or companies to expand the reach of your post?
☐	Have you included questions or polls to facilitate engagement and gather insights from your audience?
☐	If applicable, have you added high-quality images or videos that complement and elevate your post content?

10 Types of LinkedIn Posts to Enhance Your Personal Brand

Establishing a strong personal brand on LinkedIn is a critical step toward gaining the respect and trust of your ideal clients. As you know by now, one important way to achieve this is through creating engaging and informative content. This not only helps you stand out, but also adds significant value to your network and potential clients. Let's cover ten types of LinkedIn posts you can use to enhance your personal brand and amplify your success on the platform.

- **Trending topics**: Posting about timely and relevant subjects can engage your network effectively. Highlight news that's crucial to your clients' industry, but remember to infuse your unique insights and perspective. This provides an additional commentary layer, inviting more interactions. Avoid divisive topics such as politics to maintain professionalism.
- **Conversation-inspiring posts**: Provoke insightful discussions and productive debates by presenting content related to your industry's

critical issues. Aim to offer a fresh perspective on relevant topics. When crafting these posts, consider the type of conversation you want to create, and pose open-ended questions to accommodate a variety of viewpoints.

- **Thought-provoking posts**: A thought-provoking post is an excellent avenue for showcasing your knowledge and expertise. Focus on industry-specific problems or trends that are particularly significant to your potential clients. By offering unique perspectives, you can spark interest and pull your audience into meaningful exchanges. Ensure these posts are well-researched, informative, and tailored to your audience's needs.

- **Professional updates and milestones**: Sharing your professional growth and milestones adds a personal touch and can build familiarity and rapport with your audience. It could be a new job, a promotion, a business achievement, a new solution, or even a lesson learned. Visual aids, where appropriate, can enhance interest and provide a visual introduction to potential clients. It keeps your audience updated on your professional trajectory and displays your commitment to continuous improvement.

- **Case studies and customer stories**: Narrating a customer's journey, from challenges to solutions, resonates powerfully with prospects. Start by describing the customer and the problem they faced. Then detail the solution you provided and highlight the benefits they reaped from your solution. Let the success stories of your customers speak for your expertise and value. These narratives not only validate your capabilities but also help potential clients envision the solutions you can provide.

- **Seasonal posts**: Season-related content can tap into the collective mood and drive higher engagement. Whether it's New Year's resolutions, Thanksgiving gratitude, or a Christmas countdown, such posts can incite spirited interactions with your network. You could also leverage LinkedIn's Polls feature to solicit their opinions on holiday-related topics.

- **Thought leadership posts**: Thought leadership-style content helps build your authority in your industry. Share unique insights on industry trends, challenges, and opportunities. Your posts should demonstrate your expertise and offer practical advice your audience can put to immediate use. Remember, quality takes precedence over quantity when it comes to creating content that genuinely adds value.

- **Industry insights and news**: Sharing the latest industry insights and news will aid in establishing your credibility on LinkedIn. This could be in the form of articles, research findings, events, or your personal commentary. Keeping the shared information relevant and current positions you as an informed authority in your field.

- **Collaborative posts and other content**: Collaboration can extend your reach and deepen your industry relationships. You could partner with industry leaders to generate posts offering unique perspectives. Sharing content from these thought leaders and tagging them can stimulate engaging discussions and build professional relationships. You will find a section dedicated to this topic later in this chapter.

- **Highlighting company culture and values**: Showcasing your company culture and values can create a sense of community and attract like-minded professionals. Whether it's an employee success story, company achievements, or charitable initiatives that align with your values, sharing these can boost brand awareness and bolster your company's reputation.

By effectively diversifying your LinkedIn posts, you can strengthen your personal brand, engage your audience more effectively, and become seen as a trusted authority. Remember, the goal of your LinkedIn presence should be to add value to your network while establishing meaningful professional connections.

Videos, LinkedIn Live, and Audio Events

While it's true that your LinkedIn marketing strategy can benefit from diverse forms of content, the decision to use videos hinges on your comfort and confidence level. If you're comfortable using video, it can be an effective tool for increasing engagement and establishing credibility, since it can provide valuable insights, share experiences, or offer practical advice on topics relevant to your audience. However, it's not necessary, and your LinkedIn strategy can still be effective without it, especially if you are uncomfortable creating videos.

If you decide to include video content, consider these tips:

- **Embrace storytelling**: Telling a story can create an emotional connection with your audience and build trust. Be sure to construct a compelling narrative with a clear beginning, middle, and end, capped with a powerful call to action.
- **Offer value**: Ensure that your video content delivers value, such as practical tips or industry insights. Avoid excessive promotional content, which can be off-putting.
- **Keep it concise**: Considering the typically short attention spans on social media, strive to keep your videos concise and to the point, ideally no longer than a few minutes.

If you've enabled Creator Mode for access to LinkedIn Live and Audio Events, and you're comfortable with real-time interaction, these features can effectively boost engagement. They allow you to answer audience questions and demonstrate your expertise in real time. Here are some tips for using them:

- **Map out your content:** To stay focused and provide a valuable experience for your audience, plan your content in advance. If you aim to use LinkedIn Live or Audio Events regularly, consider having a specific day and time for consistency.

- **Promote in advance:** Generate interest for your LinkedIn Live or Audio Event by promoting it beforehand. LinkedIn offers built-in promotional tools, such as sharing the event on your LinkedIn page after it's set up. Be sure to add compelling copy to promote your event and share it as a post more than once leading up to your event. You can also share the link to the event directly with others using LinkedIn messaging.

- **Engage actively:** During the event, encourage audience participation. Inviting questions and feedback helps build a community and creates more engagement. Respond to the engagement from your viewers during and after the event.

Using LinkedIn Live requires a third-party tool such as StreamYard, Restream, or Vimeo. If you choose to incorporate videos and live events into your LinkedIn strategy, they can amplify your visibility and help create stronger connections with your audience. However, it's important to note that these are options, not necessities. You can still achieve effective LinkedIn marketing with well-crafted text-based content and consistent engagement. Always choose strategies that best align with your comfort level, resources, and audience preferences.

For Introverts Only: It's Okay to Stay in Your Comfort Zone

If you're an extrovert, feel free to skip this section. But if you're an introvert like me, you may find the world of LinkedIn—a platform full of videos, LinkedIn Live, and LinkedIn Audio Events—a bit overwhelming. Take a deep breath; you don't have to participate in any of those formats if they don't align with your authentic self.

If you're wondering whether this approach works, look no further than my own experience. As of the writing of this book, I've shared less than a handful of videos and have never participated in a LinkedIn Live or Audio Event. Yet, I've successfully built a meaningful and large network on LinkedIn. How? By focusing on my introverted strength—writing. As an introvert I've stuck with my strengths which has also allowed me to author numerous bestselling books, proving that you don't have to go against your nature to have a strong and authentic presence on LinkedIn.

Let's make this clear: success on LinkedIn doesn't require you to step out of your comfort zone into the realm of videos, LinkedIn Live, or Audio Events. While these formats can be engaging, they're not mandatory for building a strong LinkedIn presence. Your written content, your thoughtful responses, and your 1:1 connections can speak just as loudly, if not louder, in portraying your personal brand.

While we're on this subject, let's look at several more myths about effective social media.

MYTH: Personal branding requires constant self-promotion.

REALITY: Introverts can excel at "soft promotion." Share articles, trends, or news that align with your professional interests. By adding your unique perspective to these shares, you subtly communicate your expertise without a glaring spotlight.

MYTH: Only the loudest voices get heard.

REALITY: In a sea of noise, well thought out and insightful content can be a breath of fresh air. Introverts often bring depth to topics and conversations, which can resonate on a platform thirsty for meaningful dialogue. Research shows that deeper, more thoughtful content tends to generate meaningful and lasting engagement.

MYTH: You must post content daily to make an impact.

REALITY: Consistency is more about quality than frequency. A few insightful posts a month can be more impactful than daily posts that don't offer much value.

Creating Collaborative Content

Collaborative content is any form of content created with the joint effort of two or more individuals or organizations. This can range from blog posts and articles to webinars, podcasts, and social media posts. The purpose is to blend unique perspectives, insights, and expertise to produce richer, more comprehensive material. The end result is content that provides more value to the audience and has the potential for greater reach and impact. This strategy is effective across various platforms, but its impact is particularly amplified on LinkedIn, thanks to unique features like tagging that enable exponential reach and engagement.

Consider the types of collaborative content that would resonate most with your audience and identify potential partners for your next project.

Why LinkedIn's Tagging is a Game-changer

- **Instant notifications**: As soon as you tag someone, LinkedIn notifies that individual and offers them an immediate chance to see and engage with the post.
- **Secondary reach**: The tagged individual's connections may also see the post in their feed, increasing its visibility significantly beyond your own network. This is especially impactful if you're tagging professionals with a large following.
- **Algorithmic boost**: Higher engagement rates, partly driven by the tagged individuals and their networks interacting with your post, can lead LinkedIn's algorithm to feature your content more prominently. This can result in even greater organic reach.

Strategic Considerations for Tagging on LinkedIn

- **Quality over quantity**: Tag only the most relevant people and only when they have in some way contributed to the content you are sharing. Do not tag for the sake of tagging, and avoid excessive tagging, as it comes off as spammy and devalues your post.
- **Informed consent**: Always seek approval from the people you intend to tag. This is not only courteous but also necessary to comply with LinkedIn's guidelines and community etiquette.
- **Timing is key**: Coordinate with your collaborators on the best time to post and tag, maximizing the chances that both your networks are most active.
- **Engagement loop**: After tagging, keep an eye on the post to engage with comments or questions promptly, further fueling the post's visibility through sustained interaction.

Review your LinkedIn connections and identify individuals whose network and expertise align with your content. Reach out to them to discuss collaborative opportunities.

Tips, Tactics, and Strategies for Creating Collaborative Content

- **Identify objectives and themes**: Clearly define the goals you aim to achieve with the collaborative content. Whether it's increased visibility, lead generation, or thought leadership, having a clear objective will guide the collaboration.
- **Select the right collaborative partners**: Look for collaborators who complement your expertise and bring something unique to the table.
- **Content format and structure**: Decide on the format (e.g., blog post, report, live event, etc.) that best suits the message and appeals to your target audience.
- **Contribution guidelines**: Set guidelines for contributions, such as word count, tone, and key points to cover.
- **Timeline and milestones**: Establish a clear timeline, complete with milestones for drafts, revisions, and the final publication date.
- **Review and edit**: Once all contributions are in, carefully review and edit the content to ensure a seamless flow and uniformity in tone and style.
- **Promotional strategy**: Coordinate with all collaborators on how the content will be promoted across various channels.
- **Performance metrics**: After publishing, track the performance of the content using metrics like engagement rate and post impressions to evaluate the success of the collaboration.

Pick a theme or topic for your next piece of collaborative content and identify what each contributor could potentially bring to the table. Sketch a timeline and get started!

Crafting a Content Calendar

Lay the groundwork: Determine your goals before setting up your calendar. Whether you aim to engage, establish authority, or spark one-on-one conversations, tailor your posts to meet these objectives.

Frequency and timing: Be realistic about your capacity. Posting quality content once a week? Opt for a weekday morning, between Monday to Thursday. Posting twice? Spread them out, like Monday and Thursday. Going for three? Try a Monday, Wednesday, and Friday schedule.

Types of posts: Your calendar shouldn't just be a list of times and topics. It should include the goal of each post and a call to action.

Stay flexible: Keep room in your content calendar for real-time updates or trends. Being adaptable allows you to respond to industry changes and unexpected events.

Analytics and adjustments: Regularly review your LinkedIn analytics to adapt your strategy. Pay attention to metrics like engagement and post impressions to fine-tune your content.

Plan B for emergencies: Designate "buffer slots" for last-minute posts and keep a few evergreen pieces on standby. And remember, some situations, like tragedies or natural disasters, warrant a pause in business-related posting.

Crafting a content calendar is more than just scheduling posts; it's about aligning your content with your goals, available time, and resources. This dynamic tool should evolve with your performance and audience needs. By keeping it strategic and adaptable, you're not just posting; you're posting with purpose.

Sample One-Week LinkedIn Content Calendar

MONDAY

Time: 9:00 AM
Type of Content: Long-form text post
Goal/Objective: Build authority
Topic: The Future of B2B Marketing and Inevitable Changes
CTA: Share your thoughts in the comments.

WEDNESDAY

Time: 9:00 AM
Type of Content: List
Goal/Objective: Engagement
Topic: 10 Mind-blowing New AI Tools
CTA: Have you tried any of these tools? Let me know.

FRIDAY

Time: 9:00 AM
Type of Content: Thought-provoking question
Goal/Objective: Sparking 1:1 Conversations
Topic: What's one thing you wish you knew when you first started using LinkedIn?
CTA: I'd love to hear your insights and if you feel more comfortable sharing them with me in a direct message, feel free to.

Mastering the Art of Impactful Content

As you apply the strategies in this chapter, keep these takeaways in mind:

- Optimize for LinkedIn's algorithm by offering unique expertise on topics that resonate with your audience.
- Incorporate personal insights and encourage discussion to boost engagement.
- Play to your strengths when creating content by focusing on formats you are most comfortable with, whether that's text, images, videos, or documents.
- Learn what types of content your target audience likes to consume and aim to meet their preferences.
- Develop a consistent posting schedule but leave room for adaptability.
- Leverage AI tools to enhance ideation, writing, and optimization of your posts.

With a strategic approach to content, you will amplify your personal brand, establish credibility, and form meaningful connections on LinkedIn.

In the next chapter, I'll build on these fundamentals to focus specifically on authority building through tailored niche content. I'll share tips on creating content specifically for your target audience, allowing you to attract ideal prospects and unlock the full power of LinkedIn.

For now, start implementing these key takeaways in your own content strategy. Remember, insightful and engaging posts are the gateway to building authority on LinkedIn.

Begin crafting powerful LinkedIn posts that magnify your credibility and authority with these actionable steps.

Step 1: Generate Content Ideas with AI: Engage an AI tool like ChatGPT to brainstorm a list of content ideas. Your content should connect with your area of expertise and speak to issues that resonate with your target audience.

Step 2: Activate LinkedIn Creator Mode: If you're prepared to elevate your content sharing game and post consistently, turn on LinkedIn's Creator Mode. This will put a spotlight on your posts within your profile, and help you grow your following as well as providing you with more detailed analytics.

Step 3: Solve a Specific Problem in a Post: Use the AI prompt provided in this chapter to create a LinkedIn post that addresses a specific problem. It doesn't have to be a big issue; often, the most effective content goes deep on a micro problem, providing focused, valuable insights within LinkedIn's 3,000-character limit.

Step 4: Share a Document/Carousel Post: Consider sharing any informative documents you have such as reports, whitepapers, checklists, or slide decks as a document post. Use AI to draft an engaging text-based summary to accompany your post, enticing your audience to dive in and learn more.

Step 5: Establish a Posting Schedule: Consistency is crucial in content sharing. Develop a posting schedule that works for you. I recommend posting 1–3 times a week depending on your goals and time resources. This will keep you on your audience's radar and build momentum.

Bonus Step: Get the additional bonus prompts I've included in the "LinkedIn Unlocked: Resource Pack" at **LinkedinUnlockedBook.com** and use the secret word *Bonus*. These prompts will help you with your AI-assisted content creation, allowing you to quickly and easily create content that engages and resonates with your audience.

Put these steps into action in your LinkedIn strategy, and watch as your content amplifies your personal brand, generates engagement, and solidifies your reputation as a trusted authority.

CHAPTER NINE

Authority Building with AI-Enhanced Tailored Content

Developing signature content that establishes you as an authority and trusted resource is crucial for success with The LINK Method™ outreach strategy. Content allows you to add tremendous value in Step 3 as well as throughout the nurturing sequence in Step 5 to continually provide value to your prospects.

More specifically, when using signature content pieces, you are able to solve specific core challenges or pain points experienced by your target audience through an in-depth educational resource. These extensive pieces deeply address your prospects' and clients' needs by providing authoritative how-to guides.

Types of signature content include long-form articles, comprehensive guides, eBooks, research reports, detailed checklists, and other formats that communicate your expertise through extensive research and insights. By taking the time to develop this caliber of content, you distinguish yourself as an industry leader and become the go-to resource your prospects can turn to for advice and new ideas to solve their problems.

This chapter will outline the complete process for planning signature content leveraging artificial intelligence, including brainstorming ideas, researching and developing the piece, refining it using AI, distributing it across different channels, and ultimately using it strategically in your personal outreach sequences. The goal of this chapter is to show you how to create influential content that positions you as a subject matter expert and the natural first choice for your prospects' needs.

What is Signature Content?

Signature content goes beyond a typical blog post. It's an in-depth, longer-form resource that establishes you as an authority on a topic important to your target audience. Signature content refers to more extensive, detailed assets such as guides, reports, and eBooks, as compared to short-form content like social media posts or blog posts. The focus is on highly informative, in-depth resources. Your content must drill deeper into topics your ideal clients care about. These signature pieces should be a minimum of 2,000 words and can be as long as 10,000 or more words.

Developing comprehensive signature content is particularly crucial for the authority positioning you are striving to achieve in your LinkedIn outreach. This high-value educational content helps you add value for prospects, establish your credibility, and get more positive responses to your outreach messages. The more tailored and in-depth your content is, the more it demonstrates your knowledge and ability to address your ideal client's needs and challenges. Other benefits of this format include:

- **In-depth information**: Signature pieces contain considerably more depth and substance than a standard blog post. Weave together frameworks, how-to steps, stories, case studies, and your unique expertise to educate readers on complex issues and showcase your authority.
- **Targeted topics**: Focus on high-priority challenges, questions, or goals of your ideal clients. Dig into the problems they wrestle with

in their career/business/life. Provide answers that move them closer to their desired outcomes to build trust.

- **Evergreen content**: While some sections may be updated, signature works provide long-lasting value and don't become obsolete as quickly as blog posts. They establish you as a subject matter expert over the long-term and can be leveraged across multiple platforms.

The goal of signature content is to attract high-quality prospects by solving their most pressing challenges through extensive, authoritative, and expertly developed long-form materials. When done well, it amplifies your influence over time.

Understanding Needs and Motivations with Your Ideal Clients

Crafting signature content with your audience in mind is paramount for generating qualified leads through social selling. Before ideating topics or pushing a single message to your network, it is imperative to first gain authentic insights into who your ideal clients are on a human level. Only then can you develop pieces that will resonate and provide substantive value, directly addressing the real challenges faced by your ideal clients.

Research proves content performs best when tailored specifically to prospects' and clients' motivations, pain points, and desired outcomes at each stage of their unique journeys. Taking the time upfront to understand these characteristics sets the foundation for successfully engaging prospects and establishing yourself as a problem solver.

Advanced Research Techniques

To really get to know your ideal clients, use different types of research methods. Some involve talking directly to people, while others look at numbers and trends.

Talk to Current Clients

- Have one-on-one conversations with your best clients. Ask about their job/business, challenges, and what solutions would help them the most.
- Bring groups of clients together either in-person or online using video chat. Ask open questions so they can share ideas freely.
- Send out surveys to clients and professional groups in your industry. Find out specific problems they deal with, and which issues are most important to them at this time.

Look at the Numbers

- Use website and content analytics to see what topics and problems get people interested online.
- Review data from any automation tools you are using, such as your email marketing platform, and look at the open and click-through rates based on the topics you shared.
- Check industry forums and review sites. Take note of topics that come up often to see what matters most.

By combining what you hear directly from people and numbers/data, you'll get a full picture of who your ideal clients are and what matters most to them. Testing what you think you know against research helps make sure your content is tailor-made to be helpful and attractive to your ideal readers and prospects.

Prioritizing Core Challenges

Work to uncover your audience's most pressing challenges by re-examining exercises from Chapter 2, specifically those focused on identifying problems, impacts, worst-case scenarios, and what they stand to lose. This information will guide your signature content topics to the problems of highest priority. This allows you to position your expertise as the solution to their challenges.

With authentic insights into prospects' core motivations, obstacles, and envisioned outcomes, you can craft content specifically engineered to move them through your sales funnel.

Rather than casting a wide net of generalized messages, targeting personas' most urgent needs ensures content lands directly on challenges audiences prioritize solving. Continually refine your techniques by testing assumptions against the information you gain from your online and offline conversations with prospects.

Creating Signature Content for Your LinkedIn Outreach

Creating really useful guides, reports, and eBooks is great for attracting new leads and clients on LinkedIn, and as I've mentioned is especially important in steps 3 and 5 of The LINK Method™. With some planning and setup, you can get your signature content rolling fast with help from AI tools.

Using AI to Build Compelling Guides, Reports, or eBooks

Outlines are helpful, but you can get even more from AI assistants. They can find content to include and even write sample sections for you. Talk to your AI helper about the main topics and words people will search for. It will locate studies, examples, and charts related to your outline points. This adds proof behind your advice.

Relate concepts in your own words so readers understand. Share relevant stories from your experience. Make sure to point out benefits clearly at the end. This way, readers see why implementing your advice or solutions can solve their problems.

After using AI-generated parts, comment back on how it could be better. In time, it will understand your needs and produce even higher quality initial content.

When Providing Prompts, Clearly Guide the AI's Creativity

It is crucial to give the AI clear creative direction and constraints upfront before having it generate content. The AI will produce more relevant, tailored results when you provide specific guidelines compared to vague, general prompts.

For example, a vague prompt would be: "Write a blog post about increasing sales." This lacks specifics the AI can use to craft content tailored to your goals. A more effective, tailored prompt would be: "Write an 800-word blog post outlined titled '10 Social Media Tips to Increase B2B Sales' formatted with an intro paragraph, 10 tips explained in 2-3 sentences each, and a concluding call to action for readers to download our social media guide."

The additional context helps the AI generate initial content that matches your objectives. Providing clear creative guardrails while allowing flexibility within those parameters results in higher quality AI output.

Here's another example contrasting a vague and tailored prompt:

Vague: "Write a blog post on customer retention strategies."

Tailored: "Draft a 750-word blog post titled '5 Customer Retention Strategies for eCommerce Sites' structured with an intro, 5 headings for retention tips, 3 paragraphs elaborating each tip, and a conclusion."

Incorporate Research-Aligned Prompts

Provide details of the discussions you've had to uncover what your prospects and clients have shared that they are struggling with. For example: "I interviewed 5 business coaches about their top challenges. They cited lead generation, finding prospects that can afford their services, and staying current on latest technology as their top concerns. Based on these pain points, suggest 10 article concepts providing practical solutions."

AI is much more effective when you provide it with your research, thoughts, and ideas.

Include Relevance Filters

Use AI to gauge how interested readers are likely to be in a particular topic, based on factors like its popularity. This will help you to focus only on the high-potential ideas that people are more likely to read and engage with. For example: "Rate the above 10 article ideas 1-10 for anticipated reader interest and how likely you think readers are to consume the content." Once the list is returned, weed out anything that is less than a 9 from your list and continue to refine to get ideas that are a 9.5 or 10.

Convert Concepts to Outlines

After coming up with the initial idea for your content piece, have AI help you create a structured outline tailored to different formats. For example, for a guide outline, you might prompt:

"Please create a 500-word detailed outline for a guide titled '10 Steps Top Marketers are Using to Create a High-Converting Sales Funnel.' Include an introduction, 10 section headings for the steps, 2-3 subheadings for each step, and a summary conclusion with key takeaways."

Or for an eBook outline, this might look like:

"Generate an 800-word chapter-by-chapter outline for an eBook on 'How Technology Companies Can Increase Employee Engagement and Retain Their Top Sales Professionals.' Have 5 chapters focused on culture, feedback, flexibility, growth, and appreciation. Include 3 subsections per chapter with a concluding chapter summary."

For a case study outline, you might say:

"Please develop a 300-word outline for a B2B case study titled 'How XYZ Company Doubled Qualified Leads Through Content Marketing' structured with an intro, company overview, challenge, solution, results, and conclusion sections."

Iterate for Optimization

The key to optimizing content outlines from AI is to iterate through multiple rounds of prompts. Treat it as an ongoing dialogue while providing feedback. Some techniques to refine prompts include:

- Asking follow-up questions on any unclear sections and requesting the AI elaborate or provide more details.
- Having the AI adjust the tone and formatting by prompting for versions with different styles or structures.
- Providing direct edits to an outline draft and asking the AI to incorporate that feedback into the next version.
- Requesting iterations with different approaches, perspectives, or angles related to the topic.
- Paraphrasing or summarizing an outline back to the AI and prompting it to make any necessary corrections.
- Rating outline quality on a 1-10 scale and prompting the AI for a higher rated version.

The goal is to guide the AI through an interactive process, not just accept the first outline generated. By providing feedback and continuously refining, the AI will learn to produce higher quality content outlines optimized for your goals.

7 Step Framework for Extraordinary Signature Content

Creating impactful signature content takes planning and forethought. By following these seven essential steps, you can develop resources that stand out and solve meaningful problems for your readers while positioning you as a solution.

Step 1: Create a title that captures attention and promises a specific solution. The title should intrigue readers and communicate clear benefits of the content. Example: "How to Generate $10K Clients with LinkedIn Outreach: A Step-by-Step Guide for B2B Coaches" clearly promises to teach a lucrative solution to a common challenge for the target audience.

Step 2: Thoroughly define the problem upfront. Provide at least one or two examples to illustrate the issue. Explain why the problem matters and how readers are negatively impacted. Consider including a survey or statistic. Example: The problem could be defined as B2B coaches struggling to acquire higher-paying clients, resulting in barely profitable or overly stressful months, such as a coach earning $5K/month but spending 50+ hours working.

Step 3: Map out the approach/steps clearly. Have 3-7 major section headings that break down the approach. Apply subheadings and bulleted/numbered lists under each to simplify the steps. Example: The solution is mapped out over 5 main sections: Create a Compelling Profile, Speak to Your Target Market, Book Appointments Through LinkedIn

Messaging, Have a Signature Piece of Content for Outreach, Structure Posts for Maximum Engagement.

Step 4: Validate strategies with evidence. Include real-world stories, case studies, or testimonials. Reference any authoritative sources that substantiate your advice, such as studies or industry reports. Example: Strategies are validated with testimonials from successful coaches, citing a survey showing their priorities, and case studies of $10K clients landed.

Step 5: Emphasize what the reader will gain. Quantify benefits at the conclusion by directly linking outcomes to the implementation of these steps. Offer 3-5 specific advantages readers can expect by following this advice. Example: Benefits are emphasized like earning an additional $5K/month and reducing hours to a sustainable 35-40/week with the new approach.

Step 6: Supplement with visual aids. Have at least one customized graphic, and consider adding additional visual elements such as screenshot examples, charts depicting data, or frameworks. Visuals enhance learning and engagement. Example: The guide includes a custom graphic on the cover with the title of the resource, along with screenshots exemplifying profile and messaging tactics.

Step 7: Call readers to action. Propose one clear next step to further the learning progress, possibly downloading another resource, attending a webinar, or contacting you for advice. Example: A call to action prompting them to email me to schedule a call if they would like my help in creating their LinkedIn strategy and messages, and outlining their signature content for them.

By using these seven steps to create content, you will find it easier to establish yourself as an expert, and will have more prospects willing to schedule a call with you when you get to Step 4 of The LINK Method™.

The Importance of Strategic Content Repurposing

Repurpose a single signature content resource multiple times by modifying it 10-20% for each target market you're focused on. For example, I could create a piece of content about how sales professionals are using LinkedIn to increase sales by 20%, and then repurpose most of it to speak to an entirely different audience about how B2B business owners are doing the same thing.

The 10-20% difference would involve you using the most appropriate language to the specific target audience, identifying their unique problems, and using any examples and stories that speak directly to them. If you target multiple personas, spend the time adjusting your signature content piece to each one with these small but impactful changes.

The True Power of AI is in the Editing

AI tools have made content creation much more efficient by generating drafts with minimal effort. However, simply accepting raw AI output misses where the real magic happens. As the old saying goes, "It's not about the ideas, it's about the execution."

Initial AI content may rely too heavily on complicated jargon and buzzwords to sound authoritative. (Just watch how many times you'll see the words "unleashing" and "harnessing!") But this "overly smart" writing lacks humanity. When editing, replace jargon with clear, conversational terms your audience can relate to. While AI quickly generates ideas, the human touch brings the content alive. Injecting your personal experiences, humor, and vivid storytelling evokes emotion. Remember, facts inform, but stories inspire.

Rather than a single prompt, engage the AI in an ongoing dialogue. Refine and challenge assumptions through follow-up questions to create richer output. Mix and match responses to build a more compelling narrative. View AI as a helpful colleague, not a replacement. Its initial contributions lay the foundation, but use your humanity to include compelling stories and insights, to create quality and engaging content.

Interactive Prompting

When working with AI, it helps to start with the big picture first. Begin by asking broad questions about what you're trying to accomplish overall. This gives the AI a glimpse of the full scope of what you need. Once the AI understands the big goal, you can narrow in with more specific prompts focused on the details. Break it down step by step to tackle each element of the content you want to create.

The key is to interactively guide the AI in the direction you want. Challenge it with follow-up questions at each turn, steering the conversation to craft your ideal outcome. It may take a few rounds of back-and-forth prompts to land on content that truly resonates with your audience and vision.

Together, the combination of AI speed and a human touch will allow you to efficiently deliver valuable ideas that resonate. You must remain the master of your content. Empowered by machine intelligence, you can reach new heights in creating quality content that always looks, sounds, and feels like it was written by a human.

Getting Your Content in Front of More People

Once you've created high-quality signature content, maximize its impact by distributing it across various channels. Don't just rely on direct LinkedIn messages; your content can reach a much wider audience when repurposed effectively.

Use Social Media

Create short blog posts summarizing key points from your guides. Post these on LinkedIn and other relevant platforms, and include hashtags when relevant so people can easily find them. Pay attention to posting schedules too, and share during times when your target audience is active online. Promptly reply to any comments or questions to build trust, increase engagement, and demonstrate your expertise.

Grow Your Email List Organically

Send short excerpts from your signature content to your email subscribers on a regular basis. Add visual elements, polls, or other interactive components to encourage engagement. Pay close attention to click-through rates to see which topics resonate most with your subscribers. This insight will help you refine future content.

Measure What Works Best

Pay attention to key metrics like likes, shares, comments, and questions on your social media posts. This feedback reveals which topics or formats are most effective at generating discussion and interest. Let this data guide your choices for further content development and promotion strategies. Over time, tracking performance will help you continually grow your following and generate more interest in your content.

Introduce Complex Ideas Broadly

If a signature piece covers advanced professional or technical concepts, publish beginner-friendly summaries on social media. Include clear calls to action linking back to the full guide for motivated followers wanting more depth. You can then follow up directly with those showing interest through private messages, emails, or webinars.

Exposing your expertise through diverse repurposing and distribution maximizes the positive impact of your signature works. By thoughtfully sharing across multiple platforms in this strategic yet organic way, you can naturally guide a larger number of prospects towards working with you.

Remember, insightful content matched directly to your readers' needs has the power to capture attention and open the door to meaningful conversations and relationships. Now go unlock the full potential of signature content!

ACTION PLAN

Put the techniques for leveraging AI to develop signature content into practice with these actionable steps:

Step 1: Outline One Piece of Signature Content Using AI: Brainstorm an in-depth piece of content (guide, report, eBook, etc.) focused on solutions for a high-value audience pain point.

Step 2: Develop an Initial Draft: Using the 7-step framework for signature content, instruct AI to draft sample sections for each outline area. Refine and enhance sections with your unique expertise and storytelling abilities.

Step 3: Polish into a Masterpiece: AI helps lay the foundation, but your unique expertise and voice breathe life into the content. Review each section with an editorial and human eye, strengthening key ideas. Share relevant anecdotes and real client success stories to illustrate your points. Readers connect with content on a human level when they feel the personality, empathy, and voice of the author. Refine your message and content until it's ready to provide value for your audience.

By getting started with one signature asset, you can begin elevating your expertise and authority, and incorporate it into the messages you will send as part of The LINK Method™. Continually refine your process to raise the impact of future signature content.

CHAPTER TEN

Ready-to-Launch Action Plan for Social Selling on LinkedIn

As we continue to immerse ourselves in the digital revolution, social selling has emerged as an indispensable strategy for forward-thinking professionals. Now more than ever, it's vital to incorporate an effective and efficient LinkedIn strategy into your overall sales and marketing approach. This chapter is designed to serve as your playbook, providing you with a comprehensive daily and weekly action plan to maximize the full potential of LinkedIn to increase your visibility and sales.

Whether you're an experienced LinkedIn user or new to social selling, this chapter aims to empower you with the essential tools, techniques, and roadmap to excel on LinkedIn. I'll dive into the actions required to expand your reach, build strong relationships with prospects, and land more clients.

The LINK Method™ : A Recap

The cornerstone of your social selling strategy is The LINK Method™. This five-step method transforms a simple connection acceptance into booked appointments, driving your lead generation success on LinkedIn. I dissected these five steps in detail in Chapter 7, but let's quickly revisit them.

Step 1: Connect—This initial step involves extending a personalized connection request to prospects. The personalization aspect is crucial, as it significantly enhances the chances of your request being accepted.

Step 2: Conversation—After securing the connection, the focus shifts to initiating a conversation, ideally centered around a non-invasive question focused on the interests of your prospects. This approach paves the way for meaningful interactions and rapport building by having a two-way dialogue.

Step 3: Add Value—In this step, your mission is to present the prospect with a resource that aligns with their unique needs and challenges. Regardless of the type of content, the focus should be on catering to the prospect's industry and key issues. By offering them such a personalized resource, you are offering value in advance of trying to book an appointment with them.

Step 4: Book Appointment—Having established rapport and conveyed your value, it's time to propose a call or meeting. The emphasis should be on the benefits your prospect will gain from this interaction, rather than a pitch about your product or service. Keeping their interests, challenges, or desires at the forefront enhances your chances of securing an appointment. It is only then that you can have a sales conversation.

Step 5: Nurture—The concluding step involves maintaining contact with your prospect, and continually providing value. Whether you're sharing relevant and informative content or inquiring about their well-being, you are continuing to nurture the relationship to keep the prospect engaged, priming them for a future sale.

Following The LINK Method™ empowers you to build strong relationships with your ideal clients and drive long-term business growth. Remember, social selling isn't a one-off tactic but a sustained effort. With this proven method in your arsenal, you are well-equipped to navigate LinkedIn and achieve outstanding success.

LinkedIn Social Selling Action Plan

The key to getting results is following an action plan. This will be essential to incorporate the consistency needed to succeed at social selling. The action plan you will follow will differ if you are using a free LinkedIn account, Premium Business, or Sales Navigator.

With Sales Navigator you have many additional options such as setting up personas, creating a multitude of searches for leads or accounts, and saving your best searches. You can save the leads or accounts you want to follow, and create lead lists to track where each person is in The LINK Method™ message sequence.

If you are not using Sales Navigator, tracking leads through the messaging process will be more labor intensive, and will either require using a third-party CRM tool or manual tracking using a spreadsheet.

Here are the activities that make up your daily social selling action plan.

1. Review alerts for leads and accounts
- **Sales Navigator:** Start your day by checking the alerts for updates on the leads and accounts you're following. Utilize these updates as opportunities for engagement.
- **Free/Premium:** Review your LinkedIn notifications and manually visit the profiles of leads and companies you're interested in to see any new activity. Use this as a basis for your outreach.

2. Check saved searches
- **Sales Navigator:** Regularly review your Saved Searches to identify potential leads that fit your ideal client profile.
- **Free/Premium:** Use LinkedIn's basic search functionality to find new leads.

3. Send the connection request message (Step 1) to prospects you have found in your search

- **Sales Navigator:** After reviewing your Saved Searches, send a personalized connection request to the prospects you've identified, and update your lead list.
- **Free/Premium:** After finding a prospect you want to connect with, send your personalized connection request and track that in your CRM or spreadsheet.

4. Send the conversation initiator message (Step 2)

- **Both Versions:** Once your connection request is accepted, send a follow-up message within 3–5 days to initiate a conversation. Update your lead list accordingly if using Sales Navigator, or track manually if you are not.

5. Share the value-adding message (Step 3)

- **Both Versions:** About two weeks after the previous interaction, send a value-adding message. Update your lead list accordingly if using Sales Navigator, or track manually if you are not.

6. Offer the appointment booking message (Step 4)

- **Both Versions:** Roughly two weeks after your last message, send your message to propose a meeting. Update your lead list accordingly if using Sales Navigator, or track manually if you are not.

7. Deliver the nurturing message (Step 5)

- **Both Versions:** After a few months, re-engage with your leads by sending a nurturing message. Update your lead list accordingly if using Sales Navigator, or track manually if you are not.

8. Accept and respond to connection requests

- **Both Versions:** Make it a habit to promptly accept incoming connection requests from prospects and initiate meaningful conversations.

9. Acknowledge replies/messages received

- **Sales Navigator:** Note that Sales Navigator has its own inbox. Regularly check both your LinkedIn and Sales Navigator inboxes.
- **Free/Premium:** Keep an eye on your LinkedIn inbox and ensure prompt responses.

10. Stay active on your LinkedIn feed

- **Both Versions:** Regularly interact with relevant posts within your network. This keeps you visible and helps you establish familiarity and rapport.

11. Monitor profile views

- **Both Versions:** Check who has viewed your profile and consider reaching out if they fit your target audience.

12. Track post/content engagement

- **Both Versions:** Monitor engagement levels on your posts and make sure to interact with commenters to encourage further visibility.

13. Share engaging posts

- **Both Versions:** Share a mix of original and curated content that adds value for your audience 1-3 times per week based on your goals. Use LinkedIn's built-in scheduler to post at optimal times when your followers are most active.

14. Review notifications

- **Both Versions:** Routinely check your notifications for any new engagement opportunities.

15. Assess engagement on Smart Link content

- **Sales Navigator:** If you're using the Advanced or Advanced Plus versions, track engagement on your Smart Link content.
- **Free/Premium:** This feature is not available. However, you can still manually track how people engage with the content you share by monitoring likes, comments, reposts, and interactions in one-to-one messages.

I've included this action plan in a downloadable chart format within the "LinkedIn Unlocked: Resource Pack" to make it easy to follow. This resource pack is available for download at **LinkedinUnlockedBook.com** by using the secret word *Bonus.*

Weekly or As-Needed Action Plan

There are other activities that are only required on a weekly or as-needed basis. They include:

- **Refresh content in Featured section:** Ensure your Featured section on your LinkedIn profile stays updated with new content that demonstrates your expertise and industry knowledge. Refreshing this section regularly is a compelling way to engage your audience and attract potential clients by illustrating your relevant work and thought leadership content.
- **Engage your audience with newsletters, LinkedIn Live, or LinkedIn Audio Events:** Depending on your business type and audience needs, consider creating a recurring engagement event like a weekly/bi-weekly/monthly newsletter, a LinkedIn Live session, or a LinkedIn Audio Event. These activities allow you to continuously engage your audience, provide value, and showcase your expertise. Schedule these according to your audience's preferences and your own availability to ensure maximum reach and interaction.

- **Analyze content analytics:** Frequently review your content analytics, including post impressions, profile views, total followers, and search appearances. This data provides insights into your LinkedIn activity performance, enabling you to identify trends and patterns, assess content reach and engagement, and track your professional network's growth. These insights can inform data-driven decisions to refine your content strategy and effectively target your audience.

- **Create new saved searches as needed if you are using Sales Navigator:** As your social selling strategies evolve and new opportunities surface, you may need to create new saved searches in Sales Navigator. This ensures you stay updated with relevant prospects and industry developments. Regularly refining your saved searches ensures you continually focus on the most relevant leads and stay proactive in your sales efforts.

- **Review your Social Selling Index score:** It's beneficial to occasionally check your SSI score. Remember, what gets measured gets improved. Find your score in Sales Navigator or at: https://www.linkedin.com/sales/ssi. A score of 70+ indicates effective usage of LinkedIn and Sales Navigator. However, don't become overly fixated on your score. The primary focus should always be improving your profile, sharing valuable content, and identifying, connecting with, and building relationships with your prospects.

Key Performance Indicators for Social Selling

To achieve success in social selling, it's important to track and measure your key performance indicators. KPIs are the milestones you want to hit with your social selling efforts. By keeping track and analyzing these KPIs, you can discover where you can up your game and tailor your social selling plan to perfection.

First off, you need to pinpoint what you're aiming for with your social selling strategy and access the data to see if you're on track. Here are some social selling KPIs you might want to monitor that track both your activity and results:

- Number of messages sent
- Number of offline conversations
- Number of new connections and followers
- Increase in quality of connections and followers
- Number of people engaging with content
- Number of impressions from posts and shared content
- Increase in sales pipeline
- Increase in deal sizes
- Close rate of sales pipeline
- Number of accounts and contacts followed
- Social Selling Index score

Decision makers expect you to bring something new to the table and engage personally—and that's where social selling shines. LinkedIn is a platform where you can build trust and relationships with your ideal clients. By consistently interacting with your audience, you'll become a familiar and trusted choice for them when they're ready for your solution.

Favorite Tools for Social Selling on LinkedIn

Successful social selling on LinkedIn hinges on leveraging effective tools designed to build relationships and generate leads. In this section, I'll explore a variety of key tools available to enhance your productivity and results. Some of these are only available with Sales Navigator; I've referenced them accordingly.

- **Spotlights Filter in Sales Navigator**: This feature offers valuable targeting capabilities by highlighting those most active on LinkedIn. Furthermore, its numerous filters facilitate refined and productive engagement strategies through recent updates, activities, and shared experiences.

- **Lead Lists in Sales Navigator**: Staying organized is critical. Developing and maintaining lead lists can help track your ongoing communication with prospects, ensuring that each interaction is timely and meaningful. Lead lists also allow you to easily track where you are in The LINK Method™ message sequence and when it's time to send the next message.

- **Adding Notes to Leads in Sales Navigator**: Adding notes about conversations with prospects and clients within Sales Navigator can keep your engagement strategy focused and efficient. If you're using Sales Navigator Advanced Plus with CRM integration, you can conveniently log notes directly into your CRM system.

- **Document/Carousel Posts**: These posts command a significant amount of attention in the newsfeed, leading viewers through an informative journey. To create engaging document posts, you can upload documents and whitepapers, or convert your posts into PDFs.

- **LinkedIn Mobile App**: The LinkedIn mobile app allows for seamless monitoring of notifications, post engagements, and connection requests. It's an ideal tool for maintaining immediate contact with new and existing connections.

- **Sales Navigator Mobile App**: For professionals on the move, this app offers access to Lead and Account lists, and allows monitoring of Smart Link engagements, ensuring you are always ready for business, regardless of location.

- **Voice Messages on LinkedIn**: Voice messages can bring a personal touch and enhance communication. However, it's best to only use this feature after some initial engagement with prospects.

- **Smart Links (Sales Navigator Advanced and Advanced Plus)**: Smart Links offer the capability to track engagement on shared content, leading to more effective follow-ups.

- **LinkedIn Newsletter**: Establishing a LinkedIn newsletter can help you position yourself as an industry authority, share valuable content with connections and subscribers, and nurture relationships. It's an excellent tool for maintaining visibility and generating leads. This feature is automatically available when you have enabled Creator Mode.

- **ChatGPT, Bing Chat, Claude-2, Google Bard**: The integration of AI tools such as ChatGPT and others are extremely beneficial for content creation and personalizing messages, and can significantly improve your communication. The effectiveness of these tools is directly proportional to the quality of the prompts provided and the time you take to edit what the AI has generated.

- **Otter.ai or Other Transcription Apps**: If you are more comfortable with verbal communication, transcription apps like Otter.ai can help. You can record your spoken message, transcribe it using the app, edit it, and then send it as a written message. This method can also be used for creating posts on LinkedIn, and is effectively for creating detailed prompts for AI.

Each of these tools plays a vital role in streamlining your social selling process, promoting efficiency, and increasing your opportunities for success.

Additional LinkedIn Features to Consider

Beyond the core LinkedIn functionalities covered in this book, there are a few additional features that can further amplify your authority and reach:

- **LinkedIn Events:** This tool allows you to create virtual events such as LinkedIn Live or Audio Events, as well as create and share an external link to an event you are hosting outside of LinkedIn such as a webinar or an in-person event. Hosting events is a great way to share ideas, spark discussions, and connect with your target audience. Events are an interactive way to engage prospects.
- **LinkedIn Company Pages:** If you are a business owner, creating a LinkedIn company page gives your brand an official presence on LinkedIn to promote products/services and distribute content, and makes you appear much more professional.
- **LinkedIn Groups**: Joining and participating in relevant industry groups expands your reach, and can provide exposure to new prospects. Vet groups to ensure there is an active community before joining.

A Word of Caution Regarding Message Automation

You might notice that I've refrained from endorsing any automation tools for messaging. This is a conscious choice, informed by the significant risks these tools pose to your credibility. Resorting to automated outreach and messages is a shortcut that often leads to being perceived as a spammer, rather than a genuine and credible contact.

A case in point involves a training session I once led for a well-known technology company, where I met one of their sales professionals. This individual was using a popular automation tool, sending hundreds of messages weekly with high expectations. To his dismay, the prospects weren't responsive to his automated communication. Instead, his credibility suffered.

Eventually he adopted The LINK Method™ and transitioned to a more personalized approach, the difference was striking. He started noticing an increase in accepted connection requests, responses to his messages, and even secured appointments. Regrettably, the consequence of his previous approach meant having to remove numerous prospects from his target list, who had ignored him following the receiving of spam-like automated messages.

This highlights the significance of sending personalized messages that display a deep understanding of your prospect's needs. By doing so, you not only generate leads but also establish credibility. Remember, humans crave feeling valued and listened to, and personalized communication is the only way to achieve that.

Stepping into Action: It's All Mapped Out for You!

Let's pause for a moment and take in all the pieces I've put together in this chapter. Imagine social selling on LinkedIn as a friendly neighborhood barbeque—you're there to mingle, connect, and make meaningful conversation. And those handy tools we've explored? Consider them your secret ingredients to spice up the party!

These are more than just digital gimmicks; they're your trusty sidekicks, here to help you win hearts, minds, and business opportunities. Equipped with these allies, you are well-prepared to stand out in the crowd, spark interesting dialogues, and attract a lot more clients.

The big idea here? It's not just about getting more clients; it's about making your prospects feel truly acknowledged and valued. Each interaction you have is an invaluable chance to reflect your understanding of their needs. And when people feel understood, they're far more likely to choose to do business with you.

But remember, social selling is a journey, not a destination. It's important to stay flexible, keep an eye on your KPIs, and continually fine-tune your strategy. Perfection is not expected, but continuous improvement is the game-changer.

Let's put these words into action! I've painted the big picture of social selling on LinkedIn, filled your toolbox with effective strategies, and revealed insights about engaging your prospects. Now, it's your turn to jump into the driver's seat. Let's break it down into three straightforward steps:

Step 1: Customize Your Action Plan: Examine the action plan presented in this chapter and adjust it to suit your preferences and your chosen LinkedIn subscription. Modify, enhance, or omit elements to ensure it resonates with your unique style, requirements, and goals. I've incorporated these action plans into easy-to-reference charts within the "LinkedIn Unlocked: Resource Pack." These, along with other tools mentioned in this book, are available for you to print or digitally store for immediate access. Get your resources at **LinkedinUnlockedBook.com** by using the secret word ***Bonus.***

Step 2: Define Your KPIs: Likewise, review the key performance indicators I've discussed. They are there to guide you, but it's essential to adjust them according to your specific goals and metrics. What matters most is that these KPIs reflect what success looks like for you with social selling.

Step 3: Implement and Engage: Now comes the exciting part—putting your plan into action! Begin with initiating meaningful interactions on LinkedIn, using your personalized action plan as your playbook. Remember, genuine engagement is the heart of social selling. Every comment, message, or shared piece of content is an opportunity to establish a connection and build trust with your ideal clients.

So, there you have it—your simplified, ready-to-launch action plan for social selling on LinkedIn. Remember, this journey is all about authenticity and personal connection, so let your genuine self shine through in every interaction. Now it's time to get started. I can't wait to see how you transform your social selling game. Good luck!

CONCLUSION

"Setting a goal is not the main thing. It is deciding how you will go about achieving it and staying with that plan."

—Tom Landry

It's time to roll up your sleeves and dive headfirst into the habits and routines that will steer you straight toward your lead generation goals. Like any new practice, consistency and focus are key. Use the action plan I've outlined in this book as your own personal roadmap—customizable for you, your unique situation, and your goals.

You want to take LinkedIn or Sales Navigator and make it a powerful tool to meet your sales goals? You'll need a plan. An action plan that you commit to doing daily and weekly is essential. The true game-changers, though, will be the action items that align with The LINK Method™, your secret weapon on this social selling journey.

Here's where consistency is key: the more persistent you are in following your social selling action plan, the better your results will be. Make the commitment to actively engage on LinkedIn regularly. While perfection isn't expected, your continuous improvement over time using these proven strategies will work wonders.

By now, you should be clear on what you've got to do and how often. Sure, I gave you an action plan in Chapter 10, but now's the time to make it your own.

First, figure out how many leads you need to connect with each day to hit your sales goals. Then decide how much time you can dedicate to your social selling action plan every day or week. Whatever it is, remember this mantra: consistency is king. The more consistent you are, the better your results will be.

Next up, it's time to turn that list of activities into a real, written action plan:

- Start by creating a document that lists all the recommended activities. You can download the detailed action plans included in Chapter 10 at **LinkedinUnlockedBook.com** by using the secret word **Bonus.**

- Then, order those activities by how often you'll do them, from daily to weekly to as needed.

- Finally, arrange each of the activities from most critical to least.

Print out your action plan and keep it visible as a motivational tool to stay on track as these activities become ingrained habits.

Remember, when it comes to sales and marketing, you've got to evolve and leverage all the tools and tech that can help you perform better. But that doesn't mean chasing every new trend that comes up. Social selling is simple when you boil it down, and you don't need a lot to make it work. Just stick to the strategies, tools, and tactics I've covered in this book, and you'll be on the fast track to success. And sure, keep an eye out for new tools that can assist you, but don't forget my warning about LinkedIn automation, avoid it at all costs. Your reputation depends on it.

In today's digital world, trust-building is more important than ever. Take the time to genuinely understand your prospects and meet their needs. Interaction, relationship-building, nurturing—it's all key. Gone are the days when you could just connect with a prospect on LinkedIn and immediately go into a sales pitch. Take a breath, slow down, and follow the steps and timing I set out in The LINK Method™.

Change the sales conversation from "what can I sell you?" to "how can I help you?" This means investing time and energy into really getting to know your prospects and figuring out how best to meet their needs. The age-old wisdom that people buy from those they know, like, and trust is truer today than ever.

I genuinely hope this book has shown you the potential power of LinkedIn and Sales Navigator. I wanted to lay out the steps in a way that was simple and easy for you to follow.

If you've seen benefits from this book, I'd love to hear your success stories. Please share your experiences and transformations using #LinkedInUnlocked and tag me @MelonieDodaro so we can celebrate your growth together. Your journey can motivate other readers as well.

Also, if you found this book valuable, please consider leaving a review on Amazon. Your experience could inspire others to take the leap into social selling, and it would mean the world to me.

Here's to your success,

Melonie

ABOUT THE AUTHOR

As a bestselling author, global speaker, and advisor, Melonie Dodaro is leading the charge in B2B sales and marketing strategies. Her expertise in LinkedIn, social selling, and AI has revolutionized growth for over 32,000 businesses and individuals worldwide.

Melonie blends her deep understanding of AI with personal branding, content marketing, and social selling. By combining cutting-edge AI tools with LinkedIn and Sales Navigator, she has created a proven social selling system that increases lead generation, optimizes sales processes, and delivers impressive ROI organically, focusing on trust and relationship-building over hard-sell tactics.

A dynamic keynote speaker, Melonie inspires audiences, reshapes sales and marketing strategies, and drives social selling adoption. Her perceptive insights on targeted networking for high-quality customer acquisition are nothing short of transformative for businesses of all sizes.

ADDITIONAL RESOURCES

For Real-Time Insights:

Stay ahead of the curve by visiting the **Top Dog Social Media blog** and following me on **LinkedIn**. Access exclusive LinkedIn strategies I share only with my network.

For Service Providers and Small Business Owners:

Stand out and convert connections into clients with our done-for-you LinkedIn Domination service. With a profile transformation and laser-focused messaging, you'll stand out in a crowded marketplace. **Book readers enjoy a complimentary 30-minute signature content strategy call.**

Online Training to Go to the Next Level:

Be in control of your LinkedIn success by securing your spot on the waitlist for the LinkedIn Supercharged online program. **Sign up and receive a personalized LinkedIn profile audit, complete with action-ready optimization tips.**

High-Impact Content Creation:

Say goodbye to content struggles with our AI-Powered Content Accelerator™. You can opt for an in-depth 4-week deep dive or a single strategy session to give you a needed jumpstart. **As a bonus, receive a signed copy of my book, *Supercharged: Ignite Your Sales and Marketing with Artificial Intelligence.***

For Sales Professionals:

Targeting mid-sized to large enterprises? Don't miss out on my specialized book, *Navigating LinkedIn for Sales*. **Plus receive a ready-to-use Sales Navigator Action Plan.**

For Sales Leaders:

Elevate your team's performance with our Social Selling Accelerator™ custom training. **As a book reader, you're entitled to a custom-tailored 1-hour workshop focused on integrating AI into your social selling strategies.**

For Event Planners and Organizations:

Seeking a speaker to make a transformative, actionable impact at your next event? I specialize in keynotes and workshops that go beyond the ordinary, delivering game-changing LinkedIn, social selling, and AI strategies. Attendees gain not just insights, but also implementable methods proven to drive significant business success.

Ready to Transform Your LinkedIn Game?

Email us at **info@topdogsocialmedia.com** to discover the ideal solution for skyrocketing your LinkedIn success.

INDEX

About Section, 44–46
Accomplishments section, 52
action plan, 11, 28, 181, 183, 194
adaptation, 88
Advanced Search, 70–73, 98–101
AI tools, 12, 148, 149–150, 151, 165, 171
        true power of, 177–178
Alumni page, 101
@mentions, 92
Audio Events, 90, 93, 157–158, 186, 191
authenticity, 15
authority, 9, 11, 35
awards, 52

bigger deals, 16
Bing Chat, 150, 190
Boolean search, 99–101
Buffet, Warren, 15
business growth, 2, 7
Buyer Intent Activities filter, 75
buyer psychology, 12–13

call to action (CTA), 35, 40, 46, 152, 176
carousel posts, 148, 189
case studies, 14, 155
certifications, 52
ChatGPT, 150, 152, 190
Claude-2, 150, 190
client-centric stories, 14
cold calling, 7, 16
collaboration, 87
collaborative posts, 156, 160–162
comments, 144, 146
company, 53, 70, 98
competence, 32
connection quality, 95
connections, to clients, 9, 10, 16, 121
consistency, 88, 145

contact information, 41
content calendar, 163–164
content curation/creation, 147–149
content formats, 146
content quality, 95
content sharing, 91–92
content strategy, 11
controversial posts, 92
conversation-inspiring posts, 154
conversion rate, 95
courses, 52
cover photo, 39–41
COVID-19 pandemic, 13
Create lead list option, 110
credibility, 9, 10, 35, 45
CTA. *See* Call to action (CTA)
Cuddy, Amy, 32
culture and values, 156
custom lists, 113
customer service, 15
customer stories, 155
customized URL, 42

deep sales, 17
document posts, 148, 189
dynamic elements, 40

Education section, 50
effective searches, 110
elements, to attract buyers, 34–35
email signature, 55
emotional needs, 14
endorsements, 40
engagement, 95
        genuine, 15
        implementing plan, 11
        LINK Method™ strategies, 131
        patterns, 27

engaging posts, 165, 185
etiquette and best practices, 81–86
evergreen content, 169
Experience section, 47–49
expert knowledge, 145

Featured section, 47, 186
first impressions, 32, 37
follow-up messages, 135
following, *vs.* connecting, 104–105
former employees, 111
functional needs, 14

gender pronouns, 44
generosity, 87
Glick, Peter, 32
Glick, Susan, 32
Godin, Seth, 21
Google Bard, 150, 190

#hashtags, 92, 94
high-quality leads, 2, 16, 65
honors, 52

ideal clients, 21–22, 168
    addressing, 45
    differentiating from others, 26–27
    elements to attract, 34–35
    identifying, 46
    language, 24, 25–26
    on LinkedIn, 27–28
    pain points and needs, 23–25
    social selling goals, 28–29
    understanding, 22–23
    understanding needs and motivations of, 169
images, 147
impactful content, 151–152
    mastering, 165
in-depth information, 168
inappropriate personal posts, 93
inbound messages, 95
inconsistency, 88
industry insights, 156
influencers, 53

infographics, 147
InMail, 64, 66, 75
innovation, 88
insights, 19
inspirational quote, 40
interactive prompting, 178
Interesting viewers, 65
Interests section, 53
intrigueness, 36
introvert, 2, 159–160
irrelevant messages, 83

job role, 70
job search, 101

key performance indicators (KPIs), 188
keyword filters, 99
keywords, 34
KPIs. *See* key performance indicators (KPIs)

landmarks, 40
language, 24, 25–26, 52
large language models (LLMs), 148
lead lists, 189
lead nurturing, 11
learn from mistakes, 87
LINK Method™, 121–122, 167, 171, 183, 192, 195
    add value, 126–128
    book appointment, 128–130
    connect, 123–125
    content strategies, 131
    conversation, 125–126
    engagement strategies, 131
    nurturing relationships, 130
    outreach strategies, 131
LinkedIn
    Advanced Search, 98–101
    Creator Mode, 93–94, 157, 166
    etiquette and best practices, 81–86
    mastering content sharing, 91–92
    mobile app, 189–190
    neglected features, 90–91

posts, 147
    tagging, 161
    voice notes, 190
LinkedIn ad engagement, 75
LinkedIn algorithm, 144–147, 165
LinkedIn Analytics, 27, 65, 89, 92, 163, 187
LinkedIn Company Pages, 191
LinkedIn Domination Formula, 9
LinkedIn Groups, 191
LinkedIn Learning, 66, 91
LinkedIn Live, 13, 90, 93, 157–158, 186, 191
LinkedIn marketing, 157
LinkedIn Messaging, 12
LinkedIn Newsletters, 90, 93, 147, 186, 190
LinkedIn Polls, 91
LinkedIn Premium, 63, 66–67
LinkedIn profile, 31
    About section, 44–46
    Accomplishments section, 52
    checklist, 56
    contact information, 41
    cover photo, 39–41
    current location, 41
    customized URL, 42
    Education section, 50
    Experience section, 47–49
    Featured section, 47
    gender pronouns, 44
    Interests section, 53
    photo to public, 38–39
    professional headshot, 37–38
    profile headline, 36
    pronunciation, of name, 43
    Recommendations section, 53–54
    Skills section, 49–50
    Volunteer experience section, 51
LinkedIn Quotient (LQ), 17–19
LinkedIn subscriptions, 59
    deciding on right, 76–77
    free, 60–61
    paid, 61–63

Sales Navigator, 67–73
LinkedInUnlockedBook.com, 151
LLMs. *See* large language models (LLMs)
location, 41
long-form content, 90
LQ. *See* LinkedIn Quotient (LQ)

mastery profile, 10
meaningful engagement, 145
mirroring, 34
mission/vision statement, 39
modern marketing, 9
multimedia, 49
My Network, 65

natural engagement opportunities, 133
Navigating LinkedIn for Sales (book), 77
network size, 104
Network with Alumni feature, 50
networking, 55
news, 156
non-responsiveness, of clients, 137–138

one-on-one conversations, 170
one-way communication, 89
online relationships, 89
optimization, 174–175
organizations, 52
Otter.ai, 190
outlines, 171, 173
over-selling, 88

past colleagues, 74
past customers, 71
past experience, 49
patents, 52
patience/persistence, 88
people, 98
People Also Viewed section, 65
performance, 12
personal brand, 31, 54, 88–89
    enhancing, 154–157
personal insights, 146
personalization, 82, 122, 131
personas, 107
politeness, 87

political posts, 92
polls, 148
posted content, 71
Premium Business, 61
Premium Career, 61
presentations, 49, 55
previous customers, 110
professional brand, 19
professional headshot, 37–38
professional updates, 155
professionalism, 86
profile headline, 36
profile photo, 38–39
profile research, 103–106
project showcases, 49
projects, 52
pronunciation, of name, 43
publications, 52
published works, 49

Recommendations section, 53–54
Recruiter Lite, 62
referrals, 134
relationship building, 2, 18
relevance, 131
religious posts, 92
repetitive emails, 7
reposts, 148
response rates, 95, 137–138
response, to messages, 83
Restream, 158
right people, 19

Sales Navigator, 62, 67–73, 77, 106–107, 183
    account updates and alerts, 115
    additional capabilities/features, 75, 107–108
    Advanced Search, 70–73
    Alerts feature, 117
    custom lists, 113
    effective searches, 110
    growth insights, 108–109
    leads and accounts, 109–110
    mobile app, 190

    personal profile, 112–114
    personas, 107
    saved searches, 108–109
    settings, 115
Sales Navigator Advanced, 68
Sales Navigator Advanced Plus, 68
Sales Navigator Core, 63, 68
saved searches, 108–109, 183, 187
schools, 53
seasonal posts, 155–156
shaming posts, 92
signature content, 167
    developing, 168–169
    framework for extraordinary, 175–176
    for LinkedIn outreach, 171–175
Sinek, Simon, 26
Skills section, 49–50
SMART (Specific, Measurable, Achievable, Relevant, Time-bound) goals, 89
Smart Link, 186, 190
social listening, 15
social marketing, 8
social media, 178–179
social proof, 10, 36, 48
social selling, 9, 16–17, 28–29, 83
    action plan, 183–187
    effectiveness, 94–95
    essential skills to succeed, 87–88
    favorite tools, 189–190
    KPIs, 188
    navigating common pitfalls in, 88–89
Social Selling Index (SSI), 19–20, 28, 187
spam messages, 83
specific audience, 144, 146
spotlights, 70–71, 73–74, 109, 189
SSI. *See* Social Selling Index (SSI)
storytelling, 148, 157
strategic content
    repurposing, 177
StreamYard, 158

target audience, 10, 26, 147, 151, 165

targeted reach, 146
targeted topics, 168–169
TeamLink, 70–71
test scores, 52
testimonials, 14, 40
thought leadership posts, 156, 186
thought-provoking posts, 145, 155
transcription apps, 190
transparency, 15
trending topics, 154
trigger events, 133
trust, 10, 14–15

unlimited search, 64–65
unsolicited emails, 16
unspoken metrics, 146

value-based content, 11
value-based selling, 14
video testimonials, 49
videos, 47, 90, 148, 157–158
Vimeo, 158
visibility, 11
visual elements, 55, 127, 148, 152, 155, 176
voice notes, 85
Volunteer Experience section, 51

warm introductions, 134
warmth, 32–33
webinars, 55, 131
What's in it for me? test, 84
Who's Viewed Your Profile feature, 83
work experience, 47–49
worst-case scenarios, 23

Made in the USA
Monee, IL
25 June 2024

60635017R00125